Steve Rieschl's Ski-Touring for the Fun of It

Steve Rieschl's Ski-Touring for the Fun of It

by Cortlandt L. Freeman

A Sports Illustrated Book
Little, Brown and Company — Boston–Toronto

COPYRIGHT © 1973 BY STEVE RIESCHL AND CORTLANDT FREEMAN

ALL RIGHTS RESERVED. NO PART OF THIS BOOK MAY BE REPRODUCED IN ANY FORM OR BY ANY ELECTRONIC OR MECHANICAL MEANS INCLUDING INFORMATION STORAGE AND RETRIEVAL SYSTEMS WITHOUT PERMISSION IN WRITING FROM THE PUBLISHER, EXCEPT BY A REVIEWER WHO MAY QUOTE BRIEF PASSAGES IN A REVIEW.

F

T 11/73

Sports Illustrated Books are published by Little, Brown and Company in association with Sports Illustrated Magazine

Library of Congress Cataloging in Publication Data

Freeman, Cortlandt L
    Steve Rieschl's ski-touring for the fun of it.

"A Sports, illustrated book."
Bibliography: p.
1. Cross-country skiing. I. Rieschl, Steve.
II. Title. III. Title: Ski-touring for the fun of it.
GV854.9.C7F73   1973   796.9'3   73-13891
ISBN 0-316-74561-8
ISBN 0-316-74562-6 (pbk.)

Published simultaneously in Canada by Little, Brown & Company (Canada) Limited   MV

PRINTED IN THE UNITED STATES OF AMERICA

Dedication

Dedicated to my parents, who first took me skiing and encouraged me to pursue my ambition.

To Norman Oakvik, founder of the North Star Touring Club of Minneapolis, Minnesota, who was my first ski-touring instructor.

To Sven Wiik of the Scandinavian Lodge, Steamboat Springs, Colorado, who was my college coach.

Without their guidance and teaching this book would not have been possible.

Steve Rieschl

To my father

Cortlandt L. Freeman

Introduction

Ski-touring is nothing more than moving over snow on special skis in a safe, gliding motion, yet this sport is America's fastest-growing winter pastime.

Maybe you have seen a group of happy skiers starting off through the woods carrying picnic lunches in small knapsacks and wondered how you could do that yourself.

You can begin touring in a hit-or-miss fashion, or you can start by talking with somebody who knows something about the sport. In this book, Steve Rieschl, one of the leading professional ski-touring instructors and consultants in the country, tells you about touring.

Steve has skied since age three and has sixteen years experience in ski-touring and recreation programming. Born in Robbinsdale, Minnesota, an area of the country well known for ski-touring, he was a junior ski competitor and became a cross-country ski racer and jumper of national ranking at Western State College, Gunnison, Colorado, where he graduated with a degree in physical education and recreation.

He was captain of the United States Nordic Ski Team that competed in the 1962 World Championships in Europe. He has coached United States junior Nordic ski teams and has directed ski-touring demonstrations for international gatherings of professional ski instructors. In 1969 he organized and became director of Steve Rieschl's Ski-Touring School in Vail, Colorado.

Steve is a certified instructor not only in ski-touring, but also in Alpine skiing. He is presently chief examiner for ski-touring instructor certification programs in the three-state Rocky Mountain Division of the United States Ski Association.

This book presents the teaching progression and the philosophy of Steve's school — the step-by-step exercises and positions to lead you to a total touring technique, whether you are a beginner, a more advanced student, or an expert.

Students are quick to learn by this easy, fun method — toddlers and octogenarians can learn elementary ski-touring skills in one day, and the technique explained and pictured can be used anywhere in the world four to six inches of snow cover exists. Wellington Koo, formerly China's ambassador to the United States, was eighty-four years old when he learned to tour. Rod Laver, international tennis star, is a former student of Steve's.

If you have ever watched a touring skier in action, possibly you have noticed that the ski is rather narrow and that only the toe of the skier's boot is attached to the ski. This allows the person to go along in much the same way an ice skater moves over ice.

The skier's equipment is a modern adaptation of gear used by the ancient hunters of northern Europe to stalk game herds over the snow. The first ski apparently was nothing more than a piece of tree that would keep the hunter on top of the fluff. This was better than wading waist-deep through it.

Modern touring enthusiasts still go after game, but now almost exclusively with a camera. The recent interest in touring and the up-to-date advances in equipment and technique make this a new-old sport.

Walking around a little on skis is easy, but that is just the beginning. To progress from there to a safe and satisfactory all-day tour is more difficult without good instruction. With only a little knowledge of the fundamentals, a person in average health can go on a day tour with confidence. Learning to ski properly is important, for skiing effort can be cut in half, and the distance covered doubled.

A successful tour is an adventure in which winter trails are skied while the body is exercised in a relaxing atmosphere. The skier should be comfortably tired, not worn out, after a trip. The key to good touring is to make it fun!

Ski-Touring Folk

I think people who ski-tour are common folk who respect and understand the simple things of life and search for them in a natural environment.

Such men and women express a way of living that transcends economic, social and political distinctions, whether they work on an assembly line, are secretaries, or direct a major corporation. These persons come to a common understanding when breaking bread around a campfire, seeing the sun rise, hearing the howl of a coyote, or moving silently through God's country.

I am with them in spirit in wanting to preserve the quiet snow-covered trail, the ice-banked stream, and the animals that live in the forest. Truly this is something for ourselves and our children to cherish. And if this is an observation of a common man, then I thank God I was made this way. For once this common ground of understanding is lost, a major part of ski-touring will vanish also.

STEVE RIESCHL

Contents

Introduction   vii

1. About Ski-Touring   1

What Is Ski-Touring?   3
Other Kinds of Skiing   4
Where It All Started   10
The Skinny-Ski Movement   12
Joining the Movement   14
First-Time Hints on Equipment, Clothing and Waxing   14

2. Getting Started   19

About the Learning Progression   21
The Practice Area   25
Getting the Feel of Your Equipment   26
Side Steps on the Flat   26
Wagon-Wheel Exercises: Step Turns   28
Getting Up from a Fall   32

Turning Around: The Kick Turns	36
Basic Exercises of the Diagonal Technique	40
Exaggeration	41
Seven Exercises for the Diagonal Technique	41
Diagonal Poling	50
Double Poling	52
Two-Step Diagonal Poling	55
Combination Poling	55
Step Turns on a Corner	56

3. Up and Down Hills: Elementary Technique — 61

Where to Practice	63
Uphill Traverse	64
The Forward Side Step	66
Straight Climbing	68
The Vertical Side Step	70
Herringbone	71
Downhill: Straight Running Position	75
Falling	76
The Telemark Position	77
Step Turn onto the Flat	78
Skate Turn onto the Flat	79
Step Turn from a Downhill Traverse	80
Step Turn from the Fall Line	82
Step Turn around Tips from a Traverse	82
Snowplow Position	84
The Snowplow	86
Snowplow Stop	88
The Pole Drag	89
The Snowplow Turn	90
Linked Snowplow Turns	91
The Stem Turn	92

4. Day Touring: Planning and Preparation — 95

Introduction	97
A Touring Group	97
The Leader	98
Route Selection	98
Snow Conditions and Avalanches	99
Snow Safety: Preventive Measures	101
Path-Finding	105
The Day Pack	106
Length of Tour	107
Lunch Break	108

Trail Skills	111
The Night Tour and Other Tours	113

5. More on Equipment, Clothing and Waxing — 115

Introduction	117
Skis	117
Kinds of Skis, Including Length and Camber	118
Boots	120
Bindings	121
Heel Plates	122
Ski Poles	122
Clothing	124
Dressing from the Waist Down	124
Dressing from the Waist Up	125
Alternating Layers	125
Gear for Hands and Head	126
Equipment Care	126
All-Important Wax	127
About Wax	127
Base Wax	128
Running Waxes	129
Waxing the Groove	130
Klisters	131
Interchangeable Waxes	131
Waxless Skis	132
When Not to Wax	133
Giving the Wax a Chance	133
Removing Wax	134
The Wax Kit	134
Technique and Waxing	135

6. Advanced Downhill Technique, Including Powder Skiing — 137

Introduction	139
Unweighting	139
Edge Control	140
Sideslip	141
Christie Stop	142
Unweighting Exercise	143
Stem Christie	144
Parallel Christie	146
Exercises for Parallel Turning	147
Short Swing	152
Wedeln	154

xiii

Deep-Snow Skills: Skiing the Powder	155
Skiing Ice or Hard Pack	157
The Telemark Turn	158

7. The Overnight Tour 161

What Is an Overnight?	163
Equipment	164
Campsites	166
Shelters	167
Fires	169
The Menu	170
Map and Compass Skills	171
Care of the Woods	174
Don't Rush the Overnight	174

8. The Four-Day Touring Trek 175

Introduction	177
Planning	177
The Pack	179
The Trip	180
Epilogue	190

Bibliography 191

Appendix 195

Sources of Information about Touring	197
Book as Instructors' Manual	198
Other Information Centers	198
Ski-Touring Races	199
Warm-up Exercises	200
Preseason Conditioning	202
Three Special Suggestions for Ski-Touring	202

Illustration Credits 205

1 About Ski-Touring

What Is Ski-Touring?

Ski-touring usually refers to the recreational — leisurely — aspects of skiing over snow. The skier pleasantly glides along, using a walking-sliding motion. If you can walk, you can probably walk on touring skis your first time out.

The key to more successful touring, however, is to use the equipment properly, or in other words, to use the right technique. Then, if you want, you can be among the growing number of people who have found new pleasures on trips off the beaten track.

More and more people from all age groups and walks of life are finding ski-touring an enjoyable sport. I have recently held preseason clinics that were standing room only, yet these same places weren't nearly as crowded in previous years.

I am seeing an increasing number of people venturing into the backcountry on touring skis. Picture if you can two young couples I saw skiing slowly across an open slope in Colorado, small packs on their backs and a dog trotting behind. Their pace was graceful, skis and poles moving rhythmically against the sparkling white background. It's a warm memory and gives a good idea of what touring is all about.

Whether you go one mile or eight miles on a trip is up to you, but you should ski at your own pace, taking time to relax along the way. This is the easy approach to the sport.

One of the unusual aspects of touring is that it is done in winter, when a snug house and a warm fire tend to promote indoor activity. Put that notion aside, and you will find that the woods can be as charming in winter as in other times of the year. A trip down a quiet, snowy backwoods trail can reveal a world of stark beauty and sharp contrasts. There is a boldness to winter landscapes not seen in other seasons, when greenery softens the countryside, and that too is part of ski-touring.

You don't need fancy equipment to ski-tour. Moderately priced skis and boots (for purchase or rental) will work just fine. Warm, roomy clothing, which you might have tucked away in a closet, plus the natural movement of the body, are enough to keep you comfortable on a winter outing.

Knowing the finer points of the sport, including technique, equipment, clothing and special tools of the trade, such as wax, will enable you to ski farther, better and easier with less trouble.

Soon you will be able to ski on a full-day tour. It can be a route of your own choosing or a well-traveled path. The snow will be your friend, and you will have learned its properties and how to use them.

You will begin your tour with a group of friends, and then maybe let a little distance get between you and the next skier, so you are alone with your thoughts, testing your body, relaxing your mind. You may see a deer in a glade, a rabbit beneath an evergreen, or a bird in the sky.

During a rest stop, everybody will get together again for a quick-energy snack, small talk, or equipment adjustments.

Then off again to explore a winter wonderland, have a picnic lunch (without the ants), and complete the tour.

While on the trail, you will have to be somewhat knowledgeable about snow texture, weather signs and other outdoor lore. Instead of being a passive observer of the wilderness you will become an active participant in it.

Also, touring is a togetherness sport. I have seen groups of people who hardly knew each other join for an impromptu picnic in the woods, each offering to the communal pot the little he or she had. Lasting friendships have been made this way.

Touring can be done on most public lands, such as national forests or state parks. All you have to do is get out on the trail. With ski-touring, getting there is part of the fun!

If you have shied from winter sports, including skiing, because of rising equipment, clothing and vacation costs, you should learn about ski-touring and why it is a booming winter pastime.

Other Kinds of Skiing

Where does the gentle art of ski-touring fit into the total skiing picture? Let's look at the two main kinds of skiing and see.

Alpine skiing, one of the major divisions, utilizes heavier skis, stiffer boots, and more rigid bindings than does ski-touring, which belongs to the other major division of skiing, Nordic skiing. The term "Alpine" refers to recreational downhill skiing and competitive downhill, slalom and giant slalom ski-racing. Alpine skiers usually ride mechanical lifts to the top of a slope and then ski down to ride the lift again.

The classification "Nordic" comes from the Scandinavians, who use the term as a catchall phrase to include ski-touring, cross-country ski-racing, ski-mountaineering, ski-biathlon and ski-jumping.

Touring equipment is a little heavier than cross-country equipment, more durable, and less difficult to manage, especially in powder snow. Touring gear may be used for downhill skiing and for sightseeing in rolling terrain. Such things as hearing the wind whispering through the trees or feeling a December chill vanish with the easy movements of the touring stride are important parts of touring.

Cross-country racing is an endurance sport requiring tremendous physical stamina. A skier uses the lightest equipment possible for races lasting up to three hours over a measured distance on a prepared track. Speed is essential.

Sometimes "cross-country skiing" is used to mean "ski-

touring," but a race is different from a hike and so I maintain a distinction between the two.

Ski-mountaineering is the ski ascent and descent of mountains. Mountaineering equipment is heavier than touring equipment. Boots are stiffer, bindings more firm, skis usually have steel edges and resemble Alpine skis. Ski-mountaineers pack supplies on their backs and sometimes attach stiff, fibrous animal skins (climbers) to their skis for going up long hills and mountains. Winter camping and climbing, which may include technical rock work, are major goals. But for those inclined toward harder work the rewards are all the more spectacular.

Ski-biathlon is a competitive, military-type event, combining cross-country ski-racing and rifle marksmanship.

Ski-jumping is also a competitive event. Heavy, wide skis with several grooves on the bottom are used for jumping as far as possible — and with the greatest style — from prepared ski jumps.

Another kind of ski-jumping is called "ski-flying," because of the distance a jumper goes. This is a daredevil sport in which participants zoom down steep inruns, reaching speeds of eighty miles an hour before "flying" through the air. Sometimes jumpers leap more than five hundred feet. The jumping hill is specially contoured to allow the skier to remain in the air as long as possible, following the slope of the hill. Distance and body position in flight and upon landing are judged important.

No matter what kind of skiing you ultimately become interested in, the essential skills of balance, coordination and

Steve Rieschl over Mitterndorf, Austria.

sliding on skis needed for all forms of the sport can be learned by ski-touring. Touring is the easiest and the safest way to introduce yourself to skiing. As a matter of fact, I know people who, having broken their legs Alpine skiing, were told by their doctors to quit downhill and try touring instead if they still wanted to ski.

Other aspects of the sport also help make it appealing. Clothing is comfortable, loose-fitting (for easy movement) and warm. A parka, sweater, knickers and knee socks are common attire. Boots are soft and pliable, yet durable. Skis are narrow and flexible. Simple bindings are engineered to grip only the toe of the boot, freeing the heel to move, as in walking. This allows the skier to glide over the snow and sightsee at the same time. Ski poles, used for balance and support, and to assist the skier's forward progress, are fairly long and lightweight. And touring equipment is easy to care for.

The sport is now constantly being updated by industry experts and the latest discoveries from related fields. Its future looks bright.

Where It All Started

Ski-touring as we know it is relatively new. The sport has come a long way from solid-wood ski construction,* cane harnesses, and leather reins attached to the tips of the skis to turn them. We will probably be amazed to see a touring skier's equipment twenty years from now; but imagine how a turn-of-the-century skier like Arnold Lunn, one of the pioneers of modern skiing, would feel if he could see a group take off today!

Lunn was a great advocate of ski-touring in the early 1900s and wrote several books about skiing. He was president of the British Ski Club when it staged some of the first slalom ski races.

Lunn's observations on early skiing have a thread of relevance for touring skiers today, and he would delight in the new equipment and the interest in oversnow skiing. But the innovative soul who first strapped on a slab of tree and chased an animal through the snow would be bewildered by the modern skier.

Can you imagine what it would be like for an ancient skier to stumble out of the Swedish wilderness and into the start of the Vasaloppet citizens' ski race, where some nine thousand contestants begin en masse?

So much for fantasy. Ski-touring probably began with ancient man's earnest desire to travel quickly and quietly over the snow in his pursuit of food. Norwegian cave-wall carvings believed to be forty centuries old depict a man with bow in hand and skis on feet. Similar data have been discovered in Sweden.

There is a certain amount of competition between Norway, Sweden, Finland, and even Russia, over the ancientness of their archaeological finds pertaining to skiing. Each country has uncovered skis, or parts of skis, or cave drawings dated around 2500 B.C. This makes the data older than the countries that would like to lay claim to skiing's earliest beginnings. It is probably safe to assume that traveling over the snow on "skis" started in several places about the same time.

One of the oldest skis is the Ovrebo Ski, which was found in a marsh in the Vest-Agder district of southern Norway. This "ski from the bog" manages to find its way into most books on skiing and is probably the most famous ancient ski. Now encased in the Ski Museum in Oslo, it has been dated to about 2000 B.C.

As for technique, ancient man was an inventive creature. Some oversnow hunters, apparently from Siberia,

---

* One of the big breakthroughs in skiing occurred in the late nineteenth century. Up until that time, skis were made from a single piece of wood. Then, in 1891 a Norwegian ski-maker glued two different pieces of wood together, producing the first pair of light, laminated skis. Laminations make a ski stronger, lighter, more flexible, and provide innumerable variations for engineers to improve performance. In the 1930s the multilaminated ski appeared. Today, laminations are used to create special effects, such as the way a ski bends from front to back. One ski can comprise up to thirty laminations of woods coming from eleven countries.

wore one long ski for support on the fluff and another shorter ski, covered with fur, to push from—much the same way a youngster might use a scooter.

One of the first military uses of skis was in 1200, when King Sverre of Norway sent his scouts out on them, and skis played an important part in the founding of Sweden. In 1521, Gustavus Vasa skied from Sälen to Mora to lead a revolt against the Danes, who had controlled the country for years.

History tells us Vasa first escaped from the Danes and went into hiding in Norway. At Christmastime he went to Dalarna Province, in Sweden, to drum up support for a revolt, but he was unsuccessful and was forced to flee on skis from pursuing Danish officers, who wanted to execute him.

Just as Vasa was about to cross the Norwegian border at Sälen, ski runners from Mora caught up with him and asked him to return and lead a revolt. The revolution was successful and in 1523 Gustavus Vasa was elected King Gustav I.

The famous Vasaloppet race has been named for Gustavus Vasa's fifty-mile trip between Sälen and Mora. The contest, for cross-country ski racers and ski-touring enthusiasts, follows the same trail over which the Swedish hero carried his message of freedom.

Finnish ski troops harassed the Russian army in the Russo-Finnish war of 1939–40. Skiing out of the hills and using hit-and-run tactics, the Finns kept the Russians at bay. Sometimes the ski troops attacked as the Russians crossed frozen lakes. The skiers would place explosives on the ice and then slide away. The resulting blast would fracture the ice, sinking Russian armor and the men who were unable to escape.

The ski troops badly mauled the Russians during the winter, but when the snow melted, an overwhelming number of Red soldiers defeated the tenacious Finns.

The American army's Tenth Mountain Division, which trained at Camp Hale, Colorado, and fought in World War II, has spawned numerous central figures in the American ski industry. Army mountain training continues in Alaska and is responsible for some of the finest cold-weather-injury research being done. All skiers will benefit from these findings.

The United States is not without its ski-touring folk heroes. From the 1850s to the 1870s, John A. "Snowshoe" Thompson carried the mail ninety miles over the California Sierra on skis. Thompson and the Reverend John L. Dyer, who carried the mail in Colorado in the 1860s, used homemade skis about eleven feet long. Both were legendary skiers. "Snowshoe" made two- and three-day trips over high mountain passes.

When the ancient hunter finished his dinner of meat taken with the help of skis, he probably put the boards back on his feet and fooled around just for fun. Maybe he tried to find a better way to use his skis. When the battle was over, victorious ski troops most likely skied joyously home.

And a sport was born.

So, ski-touring enthusiasts are linked in spirit to a long heritage of oversnow skiers: from the ancient hunters to the gods and goddesses of Norse mythology to the daring ski troops of Scandinavia to the winners of the world's most prestigious cross-country ski race, the Holmenkollen in Norway.

The Skinny-Ski Movement

Where is ski-touring today, and how did it get here?

There is no way of knowing just how many touring skiers there are in the United States, but people in the business put the figure at a million.

Every fourth pair of skis sold in this country is a Nordic, as opposed to an Alpine, ski. Unofficial figures in 1969–70 revealed that some fifty thousand pairs of new cross-country, or touring, skis were purchased. Compare that to a 1971–72 season total of more than two hundred thousand pairs. Ask yourself when you first heard about touring.

The sport has been growing silently in America, nurtured by Norwegians, Finns, Swedes, Germans and Slavs, who toured in the old country and brought their life style to the New World. Now it seems to be part of the expanding ecology movement. Anyone seeking a harmonious balance between himself and his environment might be a good prospect for the "movement."

Those who learn to tour no longer have to stay at home during the winter months, waiting for the snow to melt before they can enjoy the forests, flatlands and mountains in a safe and natural manner. And summer hikers can now take to the woods during the snow months.

Then there are those who desire an easy and relatively inexpensive way to spend an afternoon of gentle exercise, or there may be others just looking around for something new and exciting to do. All of these people will probably like ski-touring.

The "Skinny-Ski Movement" is not only a return to the first kind of skiing, which was walking over the snow, but also incorporates the advancements made in modern downhill skiing. Modern ski-touring is actually the best of two worlds.

It is only fair that touring skiers should use most of the downhill skiers' turns and stops since the first Alpine skiers of central Europe borrowed their technique from the Scandinavians, even though the possibility was good that flatland moves would send a person straight down a steep mountain in a fearsome ride.

It quickly became obvious that turns and stops were necessary for self-preservation in the Alps. Therefore, most agreed that the Norwegian technique of schussing (going straight down) a small mound and then turning uphill to stop wasn't applicable for mountain slopes. It was too dangerous. The result was a gradual parting of the ways between what came to be known as Nordic and Alpine skiing.

Nordic skiers kept the ski boot attached to the ski only at the toe. Alpine skiers began fastening the whole boot to the ski for greater control in turning and stopping. They got more control, but along with it came more of a possibility of a broken leg.

Now we have a full circle. Loose-heel skiing, or touring, is popular once again, and with the advances in equipment, it is easy for a touring skier to master downhill turns on his own equipment *without* locking the heel of the boot to the ski. The safety advantage of a loose heel is maintained and the skier can slide down mountain slopes under control.

There shouldn't be any reason Nordic and Alpine skiing can't exist side by side and even complement each other. Some Alpine ski areas now provide touring trails, and more is to come. For example, there is a move to create ski-touring areas with groomed trails. A nominal fee would be charged, to help maintain the course, and skiers would have a safe path to travel without having to break trail. However, for those who want to select their own route, skiing where nobody else has been, there should always be a place available.

Recognition of ski-touring is coming from other areas. The United States Ski Association (USSA), which has been composed mostly of Alpine skiers for many years, is turning its attention to touring and other Nordic sports. Touring is even becoming part of the elective sports curriculum of some schools. The Bozeman, Montana, school system, for example, offers the sport to elementary through high school students as part of its lifelong sports program.

Joining the Movement

For your first time out, you needn't go to extreme lengths to be "just so." Touring is a flexible sport and can be performed with most reasonable attempts at adequate dress and equipment. However, knowing a few hints can save you a lot of headaches.

First-Time Hints on Equipment, Clothing and Waxing

Skis: There are numerous skis that will take you over the snow in good shape. I recommend a light or general touring ski for the beginner. Make sure the ski isn't broken: either cracked at the tip or splintered along an edge. The base should be smooth, and if wooden, have a base coat (pine-tar binder). Any protrusion from the running surface of the ski will mar a good glide, and a good glide is what you want.

When buying skis, the rule of thumb for length is to place the ski upright on the floor and reach your arm toward the ski tip. If your wrist touches the top, the ski is the right length for you. If you are going to rent skis, the length can be six to eight inches shorter than that. A shorter ski is a little easier to manage for a beginning skier. However, you shouldn't purchase the shorter ski because as you improve, the longer ski will be needed to increase your effectiveness on the snow.

Poles: The poles should come up under the arm when stood upright on the floor and should be fairly lightweight, with baskets well attached.

Boots: For first-timers I recommend a light or general touring boot, which should fit comfortably with two pairs of socks. You might want to try on a couple of different makes to see if one manufacturer's shoe fits your foot better. Generally, you should have enough space for a finger to fit behind the foot when your toes touch the front of an unlaced boot.

Bindings: There are two basic kinds of toe bindings that grip the toe of the boot: a pin-type binding and a step-in binding. Another kind is the cable binding, which goes around the heel of the boot and forces the toe into a set of toe irons. I recommend the cable for people who wear large boot sizes and who plan to travel in the backcountry, away from prepared tracks.

If you are renting or borrowing equipment, make sure your boot fits your binding. Some touring shoes don't have a notch for a heel cable, so such a combination will leave you behind while others take off. And there are different types of pin and step-in bindings. Three holes in the toe of your boot won't work with a four-pin binding. If you don't have a special toe plate on the tip of your boot, forget about using a step-in binding. And the toe plates could be different for different bindings. However, some new boots have a combination of holes in the sole of the toe to fit most pin-type bindings.

When renting equipment, it is generally best to visit a specialty shop that has a professional to help beginners select equipment.

First-Time Clothing: For a beginning skier, the key to dress is to keep it warm and loose-fitting for easy movement. If clothing is too tight, it can restrict circulation, and if it is too baggy, it can create cold spots. In both instances you can become chilled, which isn't good.

Since to stay warm you must protect yourself from both wind and moisture, I would suggest long underwear, a long-sleeved T-shirt or turtleneck, wool shirt and socks, roomy trousers, a sweater, warm jacket and good hat and gloves. On bright days you will need sunglasses or dark goggles.

Corduroy, poplin and combination materials are good, but I like wool best because even when it gets wet it has some insulative properties and will retain warmth by keeping the air warmed by your body next to your body.

I would avoid dungaree, which absorbs water easily. Wet clothes will cool you off fast by stealing the air warmed by your body, leaving you prone to cold-weather injury.

With the above items of clothing, you should be able to use the right combinations for different kinds of weather. Your clothing should keep you comfortably warm, not boiling hot, causing excessive perspiration, nor so cold you are always moving to keep warm.

First-Time Waxing: Equipment and clothing are important for a tour to be fun, but they are only part of the happy picture. For instance, there is ski-touring technique, which very simply means knowing how to best utilize your body movements. Without touring skills you will have a difficult time getting away to see some beautiful, unspoiled country. As a matter of fact, you will have a hard time getting away from other skiers!

There are other factors too, besides technique, equipment and clothing, that determine the amount of effort expended and the distance covered. These are snow, weather, terrain, physical condition of the skier, and wax.

Let's look quickly at wax, just to get you started, and then take it up in more detail later. One of the most important concepts for the general touring skier to learn is that waxing can be easy. If you have heard people talk about waxing as if it were a chemist's delight, it is probably because the skier was a cross-country racer. For them, waxing is an art. Wax is an aid and an essential part of touring, but it isn't everything.

Wax is a special ingredient used on the bottom of touring skis to enable them to stick or hold when climbing and slide when descending. There are different waxes for different snow conditions, and they are color-coded.

A "right" wax for a particular type of snow holds the ski when it needs to be held and lets it slide when it is supposed to slide. A "wrong" wax can either slip too much or hold too much.

If you put banana peels on the bottoms of your shoes and tried to walk down a sidewalk, that would be an example of good slide but no grip. If you wore heavy shoes and plodded through wet cement, that would be an example of good grip but no slide.

The proper slide and hold is obtained by matching a color-coded wax to the snow condition, and this is what the over-snow skier tries to do. For the touring skier, it's easy in almost all conditions.

Once you have the right wax, you will have to learn some technique and a few tricks to get the most from it.

Here are some elementary waxing hints:

— Purchase one manufacturer's wax and stick with it. Waxes made by different companies act a little differently, even though most companies follow a color-code system to match a wax to a particular snow condition. Until you know what to expect, it is easier to stay with one brand.

— Read the directions on the back of the wax container to see under what conditions that particular wax should be used. Temperatures on wax containers refer to snow conditions, not air conditions. Most of the season, when snow temperature ranges from zero to thirty degrees Fahrenheit and the snow is soft, a hard green and hard blue wax will be used. These waxes can be rubbed up and down the full length of the ski, avoiding the groove. The faster you want the ski to slide, the more you can smooth out the wax, either with the palm of your hand or with a piece of cork.

— If it is a warm spring day and the snow is slushy-wet, you might want to apply a soft, sticky wax known as a klister. This kind of wax usually comes in a squeeze tube. Apply a *thin* coat to start, following the temperature directions on the tube.

— You might also ask at a local ski shop or at a ski school and find out the best wax to use where you intend to ski.

If you have wooden bottoms with a good base wax, the wax should go on reasonably well. It might take a little more elbow grease to get wax on a plastic base, but with a plastic bottom you may only have to wax the center one-third of the ski (the portion where grip is really needed).

Don't wax the groove with a running wax. Use paraffin or leave it bare. For more on waxing, see Chapter 5.

You should now have a little idea of how to get ready for your first lesson on those all-important moves that will get you sliding over the snow correctly.

2 Getting Started

About the Learning Progression

You should be ready to get out of the living room and onto snow. But before we begin sliding on skis, I want to point out that the learning progression you are about to follow is a proven and tested sequence. I have taught people from three to eighty-three to ski-tour. Most have found, as I myself did many years before, that touring can be a pleasant and exciting wintertime activity, a truly wonderful sport.

Beginners don't always find this to be the case. I have met more than one skier whose initiation into the sport was a trip with a group of experts covering a long distance. Invariably the first-timers were left behind. They felt uncomfortable for holding back a faster group and complained of total exhaustion from slogging over the snow on poorly waxed skis. Usually such an experience is enough for them to say, "Never again; this is just plain work!"

I have convinced some of those beginners to take my course and see what a little technique and know-how can do. Most students graduate rapidly from learning about equipment to heading for wooded trails. I have had good results with potential skiers who have had a bad beginning. They discover ski-touring can be fun, and instead of being turned off by the snow season, find a new and thrilling winter recreation.

You start with easy-to-do stepping exercises to familiarize you with your equipment and to prepare you for more advanced skills when moving. You will find each exercise and technique is part of a building process. If you follow the instruction step by step, the pieces of the ski-touring puzzle will fit together in an easy-to-master progression. Soon you will be gliding over snowy terrain and through winter woods — a quiet intruder in a silent wonderland.

Let me caution you not to be overwhelmed as a beginner, even if you haven't tried a new sport for years or have never tried sports at all. If you enjoy walking, you can enjoy ski-touring. Even professionals have to start at the beginning! I have taught Alpine ski instructors and ski patrolmen to tour. These iron men of Alpine hills were skeptical about the sport. They were thrill-seekers on the fast, bumpy, downhill slopes, and, like others, they had heard rumors about the exhausting work of oversnow skiing. "Make us believers," they challenged.

They began, as do most skiers, with the first exercise. Some of these pros didn't know how to do the basic kick turn. But they were enthusiastic learners. Their initial surprise at being able to coast after pushing off on a ski (the basic touring stride) changed to an eager interest in touring. They found waxing the skis easy, not difficult, and wax was the necessary substance to take them up a hill with little effort. Soon they were on the trail to hidden slopes of powder snow, where few people ski, cutting serpentine tracks in the fluff.

I told them the general touring ski with a soft tip was

good for powder snow. Their shouts of joy on the mountain were enough of a testimonial for me.

Those ski instructors were exceptional skiers, but even they would have bogged down without the right introduction to ski-touring. I cannot emphasize this point enough — technique is vital, as important as your equipment. My advice to any new student is to find somebody qualified to teach and let him give you the hints of touring that will make the sport easy to do. This will make the lifelong difference between pleasure and work. And you will have a much better chance of becoming an expert skier.

My progression, the step-by-step approach to touring, is basically the one devised by me and other members of the Ski-Touring Certification Committee of the Rocky Mountain Division of the United States Ski Association. Touring instructors in the Rocky Mountain area must pass a complete examination on all aspects of touring before being certified by this organization. I firmly believe the certification program is extremely important, and of great value to the student, for it provides qualified teachers.

Let me suggest to the beginning student using my book to find a friend to learn with you. By following the instructions and illustrations, you should be able to learn the skills to add distance to the tour, and at the same time, make it more enjoyable. You will have the chance to visit more places and possibly satisfy an urge to challenge some of that backcountry.

Many families can learn together. I have taught Dad, Mom and the kids and know what a binding effect this can have. A family can have many pleasant memories of learning together. But remember one beginning rule: take your time and be patient.

If you are parents of young children just learning to ski, try some winter games to add to their enjoyment. Have them ski an easy obstacle course or weave between ski poles. As they get more proficient, they can ski downhill between the poles, turning, sideslipping, or trying any number of the advanced downhill techniques. These games not only can lengthen the interest span of the child, but also can make it *fun* for him or her.

So, let's begin!

Pick a nice day to start, when the sun is shining and the snow is soft. It will lift your spirits; you will be more comfortable; and it will be easier to learn. Snow hard as boiler plate is more difficult at first.

If you have been careful in your selection of equipment, your boots will fit when you put them on. Wax your skis and allow them to cool before placing them on the snow. Make sure the bottom of your boot is free of snow and ice before attempting to put on your ski. There is a right and left ski, and most of the bindings are marked to point them out.

If you happen to put your skis on the wrong foot, the heel of your boot will be off-center on the ski. Be sure to check that your foot is squarely on the ski.

If you have a pin-type binding, fasten the wire bail over the edges near the toe of the boot and clamp it down. Your ski should now be securely attached. If you have a cable-

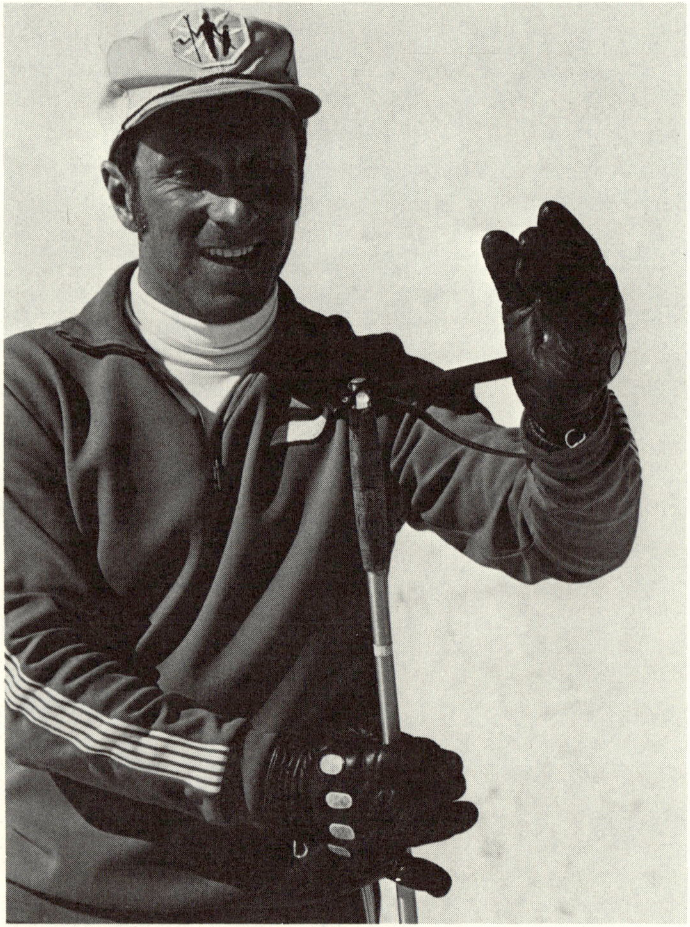

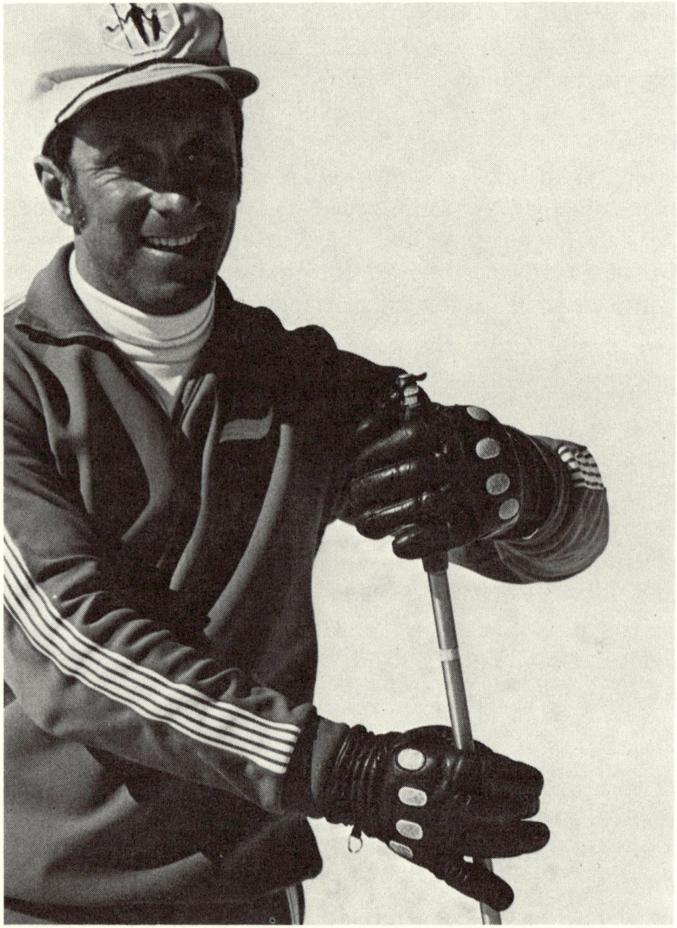

type, run the cable and spring portion (sometimes adjustable by turning a bolt that shortens or lengthens it) in the groove at the heel of your boot and then close the front throw to tighten the boot in place. Some cable bindings have a front throw and some have a heel clamp. If you have the latter type, make sure they are on the outside of the boots when your feet are together. They might catch while you are skiing if they are on the inside. If you have a step-in type, clean your boot off and kick it into the toe binding. It should lock in place automatically.

Put your poles on by bringing a hand up through the pole loop and then down over the strap and pole.

The Practice Area

Any level area is a good place to learn the basics of ski-touring. A golf course, flat field, or backyard will do. As you build your touring technique you will need a practice area large enough to make a track or course in the shape of a rectangle approximately twenty yards long and ten yards wide. A practice track is nothing more than one set of ski tracks in the snow.

Getting the Feel of Your Equipment

I believe it is important to become familiar with your equipment first. To do this, put your skis on and walk around for a while. You will get the feel of having the new, long boards on your feet. As simple as this sounds, standing on skis and performing such simple exercises as moving them up and down and laterally is very important in the learning progression.

You should begin with side steps on the flat, followed by step turns (known as "wagon wheels"). Exercises that can be done to the right and left, such as these, should be practiced both ways in order not to become dominant in one direction.

Learn these level-ground exercises well, and as the progression unfolds, you will see how they apply in different terrain. One more hint: don't worry about perfecting each exercise the first couple of times you try it. These exercises lead to a complete technique, commonly known as the diagonal technique. By performing the exercises in the correct sequence, the whole technique can be improved. The progression is like any building process: you can't have a good house without a solid foundation.

Side Steps on the Flat

Side steps are done by keeping the skis parallel and moving one to the side, then bringing the other next to it. To improve ski control, execute this exercise to the right and left in quick, short steps without crossing tips or tails.

If you are practicing in a group, leave plenty of room between each other.

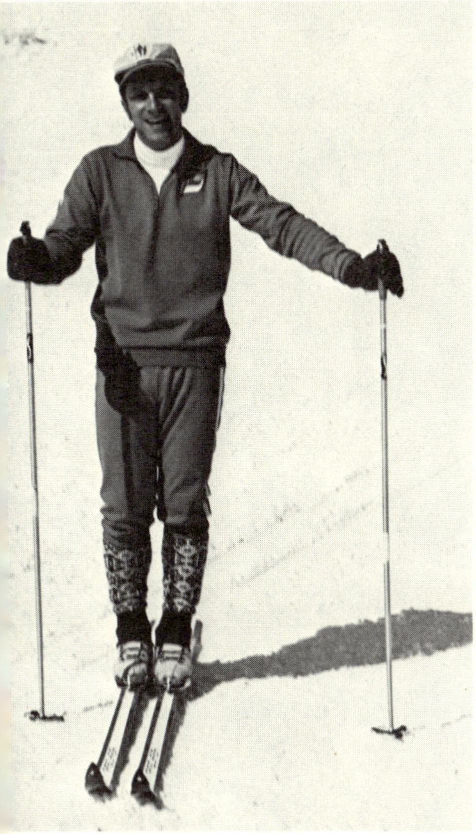
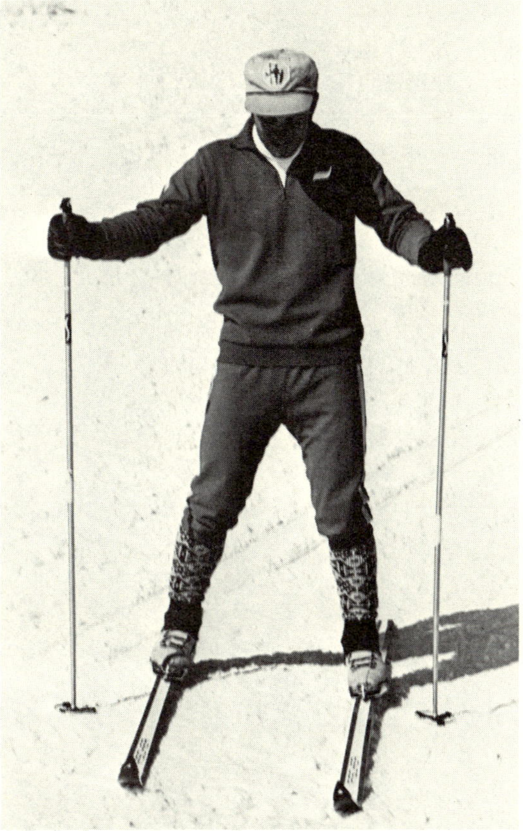
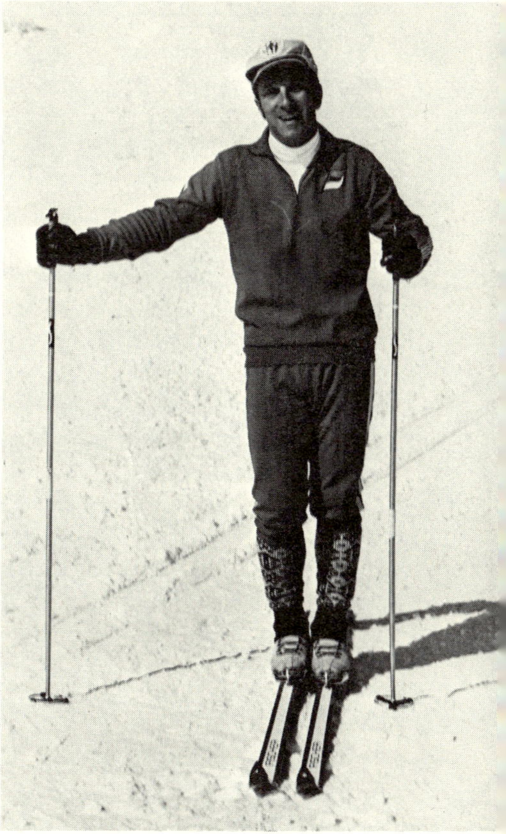

Wagon-Wheel Exercises: Step Turns

As I said before, these first skills will be used over and over, maybe not in the same situation but in the same general form. For example, step turns on the flat are essential to learn before moving step turns and some downhill turns can be executed.

All the following exercises should be done on the flat.

Step Turn around the Tails: In stepping fashion, move one ski and then another around in a circle with the tails stationary in the center. The ski tip must be lifted from the ground at each step. Completing the exercise leaves a design in the snow resembling a wagon wheel. The "spokes" of the wheel are the marks left by the skis after each step. Practice in both directions.

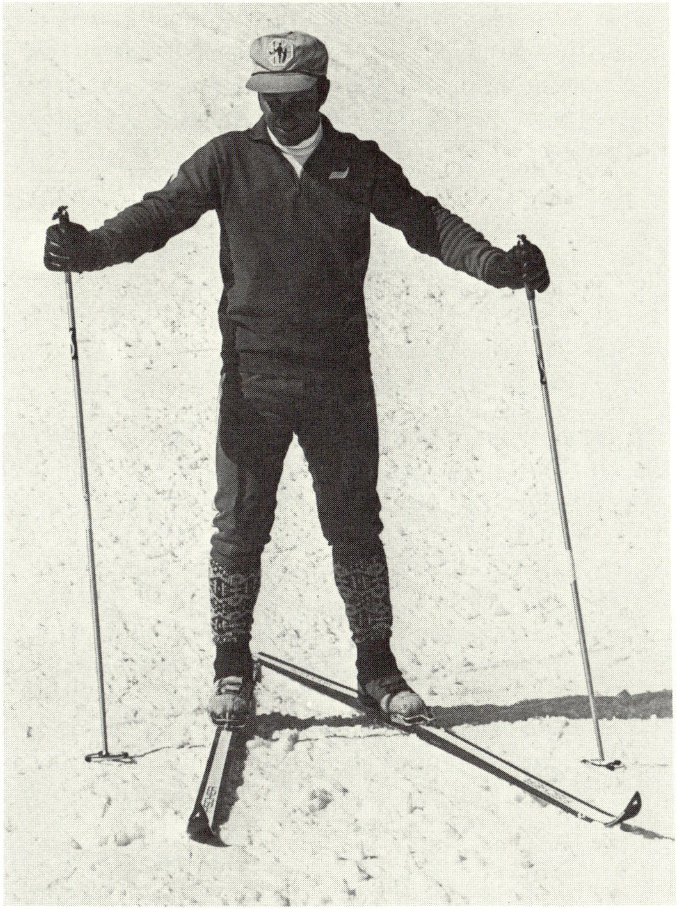

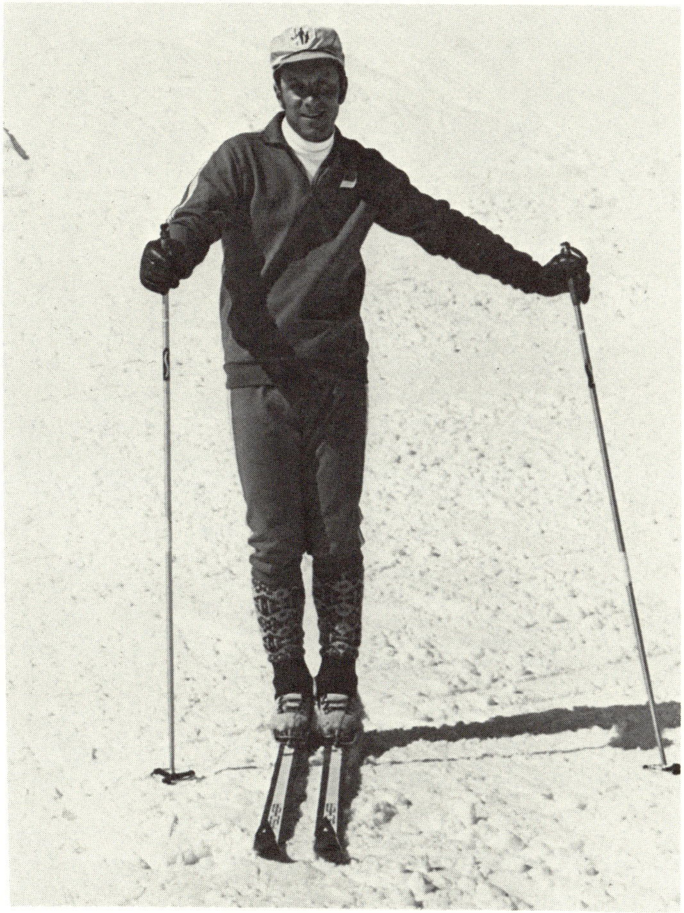

Step Turn around the Tips: This step turn is started by moving the *tails* apart and together around in a circle, using the tips as the center of the circle. This exercise also leaves a wagon-wheel design in the snow and should be practiced to the right and left.

The Combination Step Turn: The combination step turn is next in the progression; and as the name suggests, it is a combination of the previous two exercises.

Start with the skis together. Move the left ski so the tips are together and the tails apart. Next, move the right ski so the tails are together and the tips are apart. Each time you move a ski, move a ski pole. Poles are meant to be used for balance in this exercise. Repeat the steps until a circle is completed.

If you take your time and are careful, you will discover that stationary step turns are easy to learn. You might feel clumsy the first time you move a ski, but familiarity with equipment is just a matter of time.

As you practice the turns, try not to step on your skis. This is a common mistake with beginners, but don't let it bother you.

1 *2* *3*

1 *2* *3*

Getting Up from a Fall

While attempting the first few exercises, you probably wondered if you could get up should you fall over. The snow is soft and touring skis are safe because the boots and bindings provide plenty of flexibility, so don't worry about falling. Your pride might be bruised a bit but that's about all.

Begin the getting-up exercises by sitting on the snow. Now, once you are down, the key to righting yourself is to be organized. Remove pole straps from wrists, untangle skis (sometimes in soft snow it helps to lie on your back with your skis in the air overhead), and place them together on the snow.

Skis should be a few inches apart and pointing in the same direction. Next, get up onto your knees, leaning forward. Then, holding a pole on each side of you, bring one foot forward so you are kneeling on one leg in a position similar to a genuflection. When you are ready, stand, using your poles for balance and support. It's that easy.

If you are on a hill, place your skis below you parallel across the slope, pointing neither uphill nor downhill. The poles should be on the uphill side (the side closest to the top of the hill). Bend your knees, making sure they are ahead of your ankles. Push yourself up, being careful not to break your poles. For maximum support and strength, use both poles together by placing one hand near the baskets and the other further up.

1

3

4

There are other ways to get up. One is to sit on the back of the skis, and knees bent, reach between your legs, grasp your ski boot or ski binding, and pull yourself upright. Another is to sit between your skis, which should be in a slight snowplow position (ski tips nearly touching, ski tails apart, ankles turned in) so you won't slide forward. Place a ski pole at each side — not behind you. Pull yourself to a standing position.

Don't be afraid of falling: it's the great common denominator. Because only the toe of the boot is fastened to the ski, allowing free heel movement, ski-touring is a safe sport. Dr. Thomas Steinberg, head of the Vail Medical Clinic, has not treated a touring injury from my school in four years. And he often recommends touring for skiers seriously injured on the Alpine slopes.

I teach getting up at this stage of the learning progression because it is easy to topple over doing the next series of exercises: learning to turn about on skis.

2 3

Turning Around: The Kick Turns

To change direction when standing in place, use a standard kick turn, a wheelie, or a turnabout. These are easy-to-do turns that get you pointed in the opposite direction with a minimum of effort. They are especially good for changing direction on the side of a hill when climbing, or when you are trail-blazing and have skied into a narrow place that doesn't have an exit. Using a kick turn and skiing out forward is better than trying to back out, especially if there is a hill to climb. Always lift your downhill ski first.

The Standard Kick Turn: To make a standard kick turn to the right, begin with your skis together. Place the left pole to the front and alongside of the left ski. The right pole is placed to the rear, also alongside the left ski. This will allow free movement for the right ski.

Shift your weight to the left ski, bending your knee slightly for balance. Kick or swing the right ski up and around so it comes to rest alongside of the left ski and points in the opposite direction.

To complete the kick turn, shift your weight to the right ski and bring the other around and alongside. *Then* move your ski poles to the normal position for balance and support. You should be facing the opposite direction from which you started.

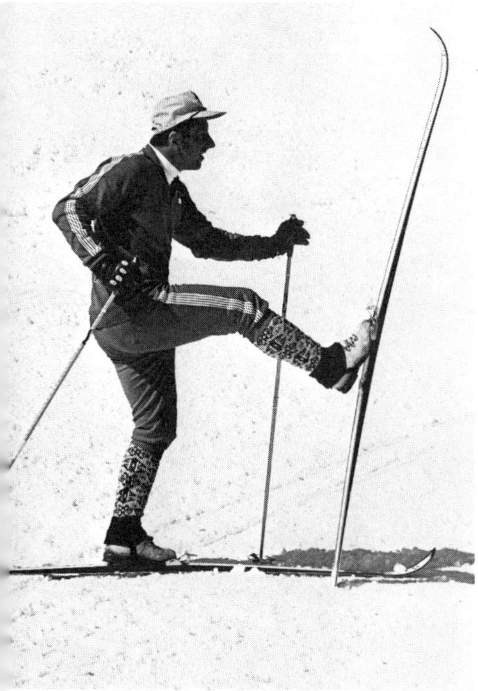
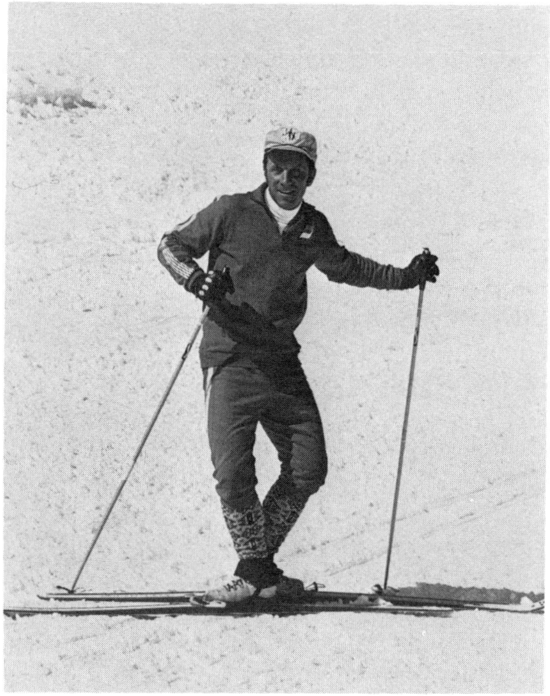
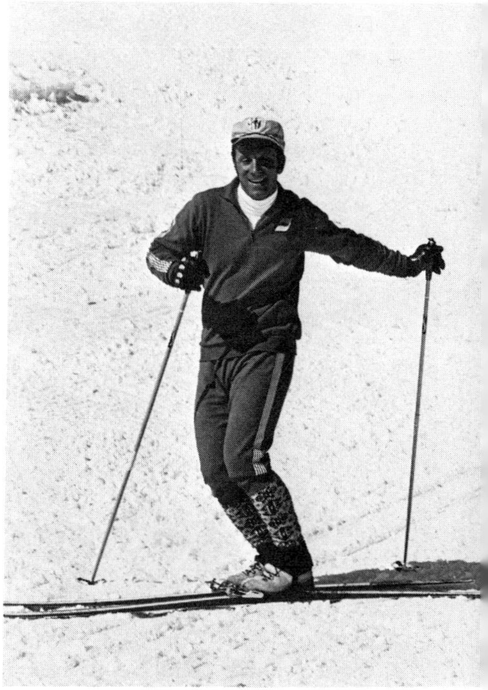

The Step-Back (Turnabout): The step-back to the right begins by placing your poles alongside each ski tip. Weight the left foot. Step back and across the left ski with the right, so the skis are pointing opposite directions. (This position resembles a plié in ballet.) Weight the right ski and move the right pole next to the right tip. Lift the left knee high and swing the left ski around to join the right. Then move the left pole alongside that ski.

If you follow the instructions closely, these turns will be easier than you think.

At this stage of learning, practice these three kick turns in succession to improve balance and coordination and to increase familiarity with touring equipment. Each turn should be practiced in both directions. Completing the three turns one after another, as if they were part of a total move, will help you get used to the length of your skis.

The Step-Across (Wheelie): The step-across to the left begins with the positioning of poles as in a standard kick turn. This time, place the weight on the left ski and step across it with the right ski, so that it clears the left and points in the opposite direction. Step on the right ski and move the right pole alongside that tip. This will give you support in completing the turn.

Bend the left leg at the knee and lift the foot high in back so you can bring that ski through to join the right one.

3

4

3

4

Basic Exercises of the Diagonal Technique

You are now ready for one of the most important and basic movements in ski-touring over flat or gently rolling terrain, the diagonal technique.

The term applies to a series of movements that propel the skier over the snow in a relaxed and easy manner. When done properly, this relatively effortless and rhythmical touring motion can increase the distance traveled by conserving energy. The technique is very helpful if learned properly.

If you have ever witnessed a good skier using the diagonal stride to cross flat or slightly rolling terrain, you have seen poetry in motion as he drives off one ski and glides on the other. He uses the poles for added push and balance. As the gliding ski slows down, the "kick and glide" process is repeated on the other ski.

The ski used when a person drives himself forward to coast on the other is called the "kicking ski." When you kick from a well-waxed and weighted ski, it produces forward movement. The opposite pole is used to help move you along. The kicking ski and the opposite pole should be extended behind you at the same time. The other ski and pole are then forward.

I use seven exercises to help you learn this important technique. These simple exercises should be practiced on a prepared course, which, as noted earlier, is nothing more than a rectangular track.

When making a practice course, make sure the track is straight, with about four inches to six inches between your skis. Go around the track three or four times to pack it down. While walking around, you will see the importance of loose-fitting clothes for freedom of movement. Restrictive clothing, especially tight stretch materials that bind you, aren't good for touring.

As I have mentioned before, each exercise doesn't have to be perfected the first couple of times you try it. But performing the exercises in the correct sequence can improve the whole technique. The progression must be maintained by adding each new skill to all the previous exercises, never eliminating any of the other steps.

These exercises should be practiced *without* poles to help speed up the process of acquiring good balance on skis.

In a class situation, I demonstrate and explain an exercise and then ask the students to practice the skill. To simulate a class situation as closely as possible, study the illustrations before attempting the exercise. Note the particular body positions, especially arms and legs.

Exaggeration

I firmly believe in using exaggeration when teaching most exercises or correcting technique. When the technique is mastered and you have a feel for the particular skill, you will be able to execute the movement with confidence and with some self-analysis. It isn't necessary always to exaggerate the final form.

Seven Exercises for the Diagonal Technique

The Glide: The main objective of the glide is to break away from a walking step and begin to slide the skis. Speed isn't important; relaxation is. Push off one ski and glide on the other. It's perfectly natural and easy. Relaxation and a good long glide will result in easy recreational skiing on many tours ahead.

The Deep-Knee Bend: This exercise focuses on increasing the length of the stride. The stride position can be assumed while standing in place: one ski about two feet ahead of the other, knees deeply bent, back erect.

The lower center of gravity will accomplish two things. It will increase your balance and chances of recovering from a potential fall, and it will add length to your stride. A longer stride increases the possibility of more glide. The more you coast while skiing the less energy you will use for the distance covered. Therefore, a long glide is desirable.

Now, try to maintain this deep-knee bend while skiing around the track, pushing off one ski and gliding on the other.

Hips Forward: Have your hips forward to keep your weight on the forward ski. This adds a longer kick to your stride and results in more glide. In this exercise emphasis is placed on keeping the back erect (the position in the first picture is the correct one), because it makes the total technique less tiring. A fairly straight back is also a safer skiing position.

Arm Swing: The arm swing is a timing exercise to be coordinated with the movement of the skis. The arm should be *swung*, not mechanically put in position. The arm swing should be shoulder-high both in front and behind. The right foot and left arm are forward at the same time. Correspondingly, the left foot and right arm will be back. This develops proper timing and rhythm and is also an exercise for poling, which will be learned shortly.

NOTE: Each time an arm moves, a foot should move. Also, each time a foot stops, an arm stops, even if it is just for an instant. This is an exercise to help your timing.

Practice the arm swing in place first, and then take your trip around the track.

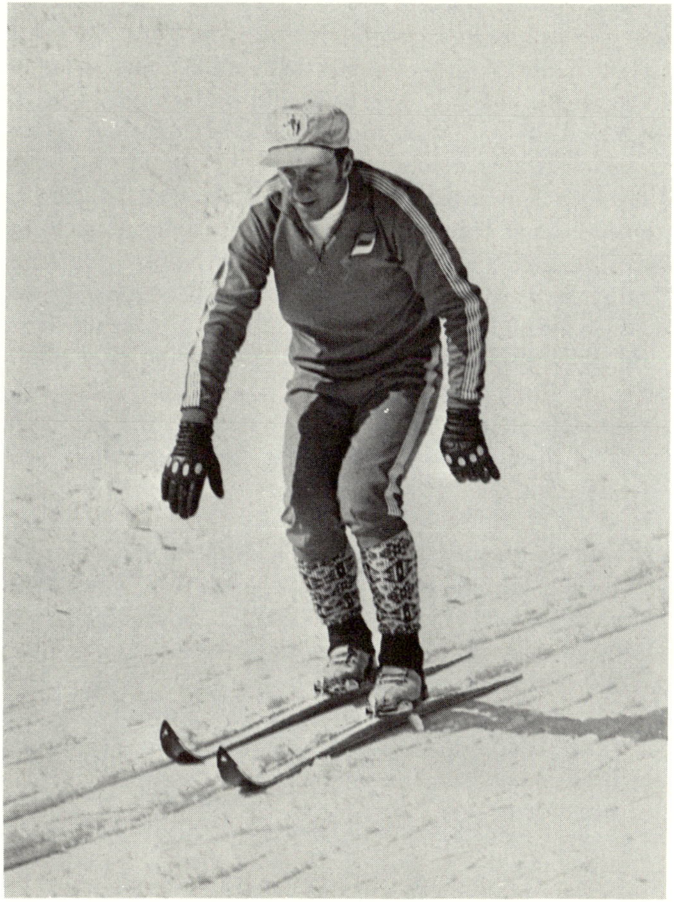
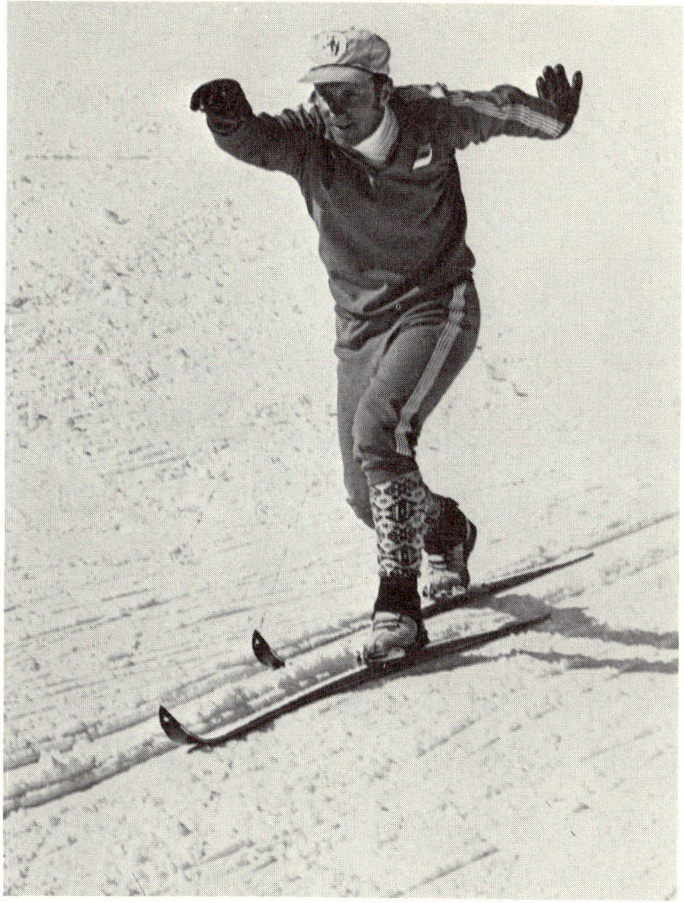

Weight Shift: Practicing weight shift is necessary to make sure your weight gets transferred from one ski to the other, instead of remaining equally distributed. Timing is important here, because the weight should be transferred to the forward ski as the result of a strong kick from the opposite ski, which is a relatively quick move.

The kick is made from the weighted ski, which should be properly waxed so it will hold when you apply a push to the rear. Try this little test to see if your ski holds well: While standing in place, transfer all your weight to one ski and lift the other off the ground. Try to slide the weighted ski back and forth without unweighting it. If the ski holds to the snow, it most likely is waxed properly and will not slip when used with proper technique in a track. The ski should not slip when motionless and weighted, but should slide when moving.

Remember, the weight should be transferred to the forward ski as the result of a strong kick. As the kick nears completion, the weight shift to the opposite ski should have taken place. As the result of a weight shift, combined with a fairly long stride, you will feel the back of the unweighted ski automatically come off the snow.

Let's review what you have learned so far: a good glide, deep-knee bend, hips forward, arm swing, and a transfer of weight from one ski to another as you complete the kick that accelerates you down the track.

wax-hold exercise

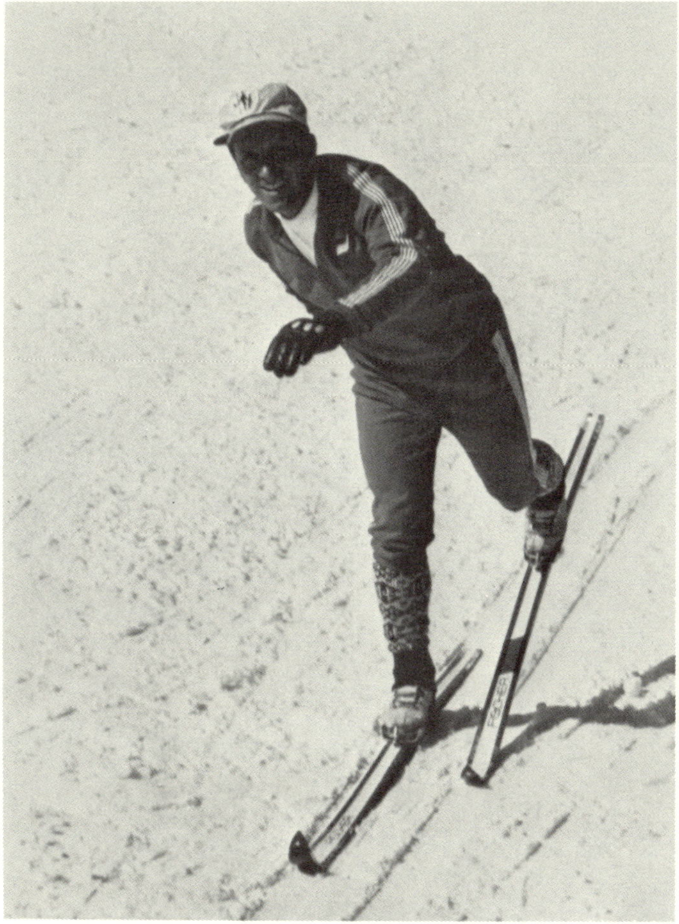

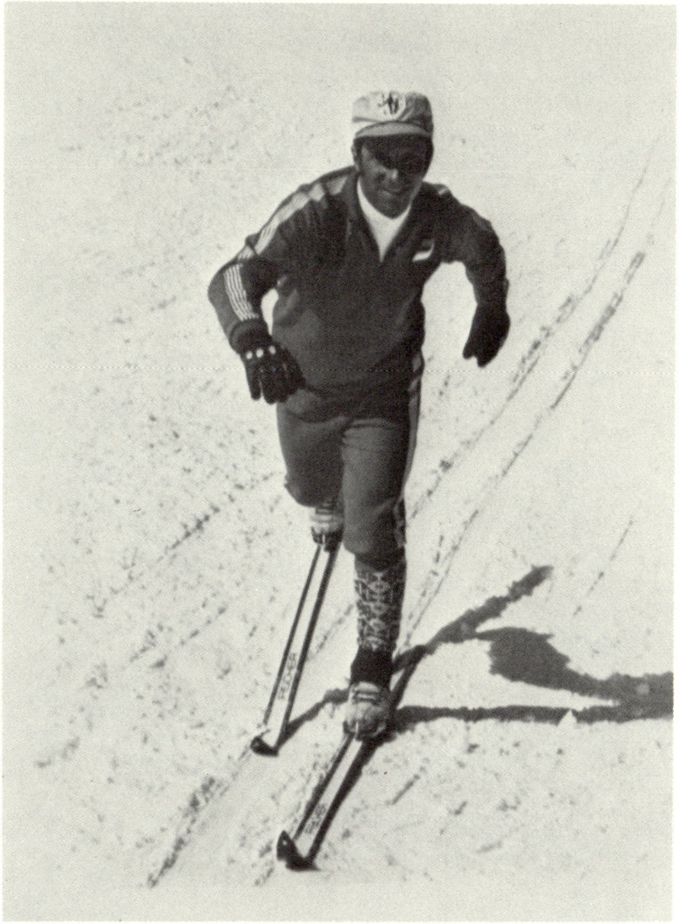

Quick Ski: This exercise will help develop a quick kicking motion. Bend arms at elbows for shorter, faster arm movements. Coordinate this with a quick ski rhythm. Sprinters pump their arms up and down, and this exercise is similar. Move around the track with short, powerful kicks and fast arm swings to develop the quickness needed in the kick.

Quick Ski–Long Glide: This movement is a combination of a powerful kick, producing a forward thrust, and a relaxed glide. The benefit of the long glide is the extra distance covered while you are resting. The next kick should be executed *just before* the glide comes to an end, or just as your momentum is diminishing.

These are the basic movements of the diagonal technique. All must be worked together in an almost floating, rhythmical manner.

But there is more to the total technique: mainly, the use of poles for balance and thrust.

Diagonal Poling

Put your poles back on. In ski-touring it is important to remember to hold the pole with the thumb and forefinger (as in the top photograph). It should not be gripped tightly. (The bottom photograph illustrates the incorrect grip.)

During the stride, the arm is swung ahead and the pole is planted opposite the forward foot. The arm out front is moderately bent and relaxed. At the same time, the other pole is in full extension behind the hip. This is the position that gives diagonal poling its name.

As you move ahead, apply force to the pole, with the wrist taking the load on the pole strap. As the kick of the left ski is completed, the thumb and forefinger guide the right pole back to the forward position.

This poling action should be done with ease, and brute strength should be avoided. Muscling yourself forward on skis is very tiring. Practice in place before moving onto the track.

Diagonal poling is only one of many ways to use your poles. Another way is to use two poles together, and still other skills provide an opportunity to vary your technique and take advantage of such terrain as downhill, bumps or ditches to make the entire trip more enjoyable.

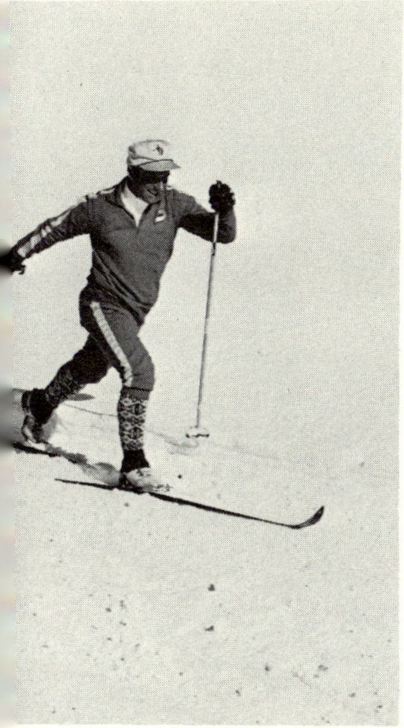
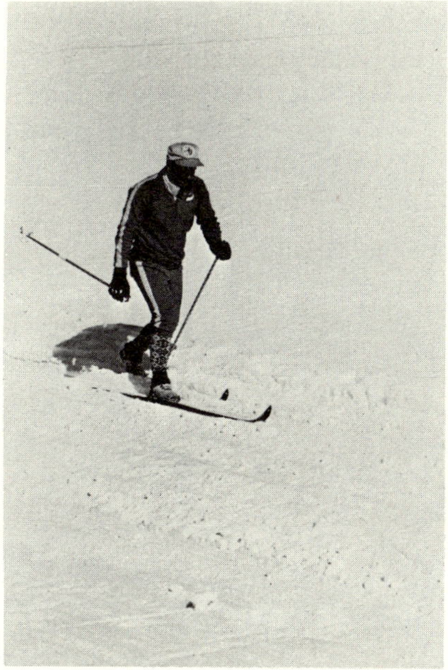
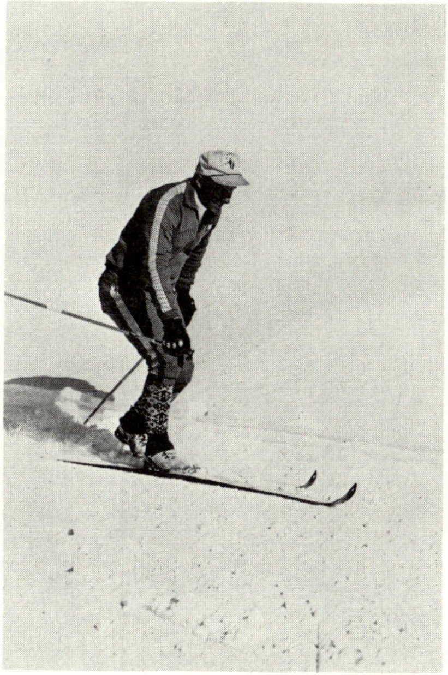
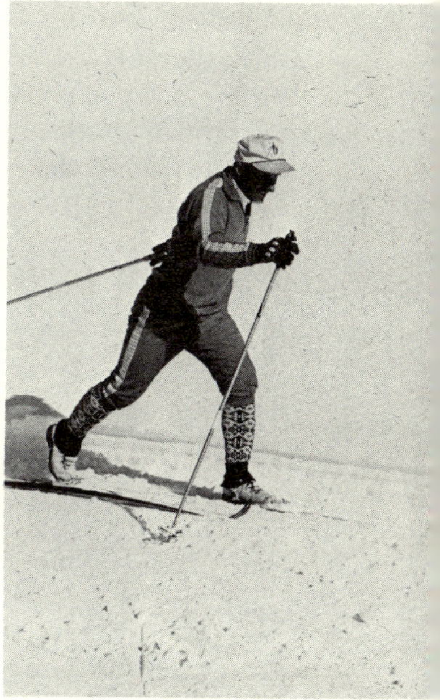

Double Poling

The use of both poles at the same time is called double poling. This variation should be employed when trying to achieve or maintain a faster speed than is normally accomplished with single or diagonal poling — if you are on a slight downhill, for example.

As the poles pass their vertical position, force should be applied in a quick, snappy motion to push them to full extension behind the hips. During the poling motion, the body should be balanced over the skis and relaxed. Knees should be bent. The upper body will bend forward as the poles are pushed to the rear.

Double poling can be used with or without a kicking motion. The variations when using a kick are: one kick and double-pole, or several kicks and double-pole, sometimes called "two kicks or more and double-pole." When using this technique, the kick is executed first, and as it nears completion, the poling motion is begun. As an exercise, touch your hands behind your back to be sure you have achieved full extension of your arms.

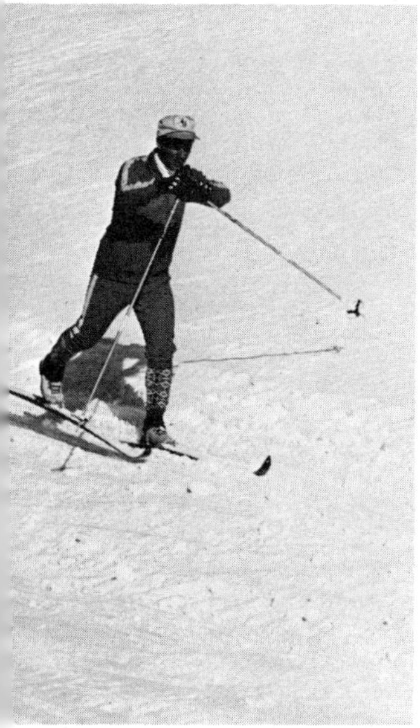
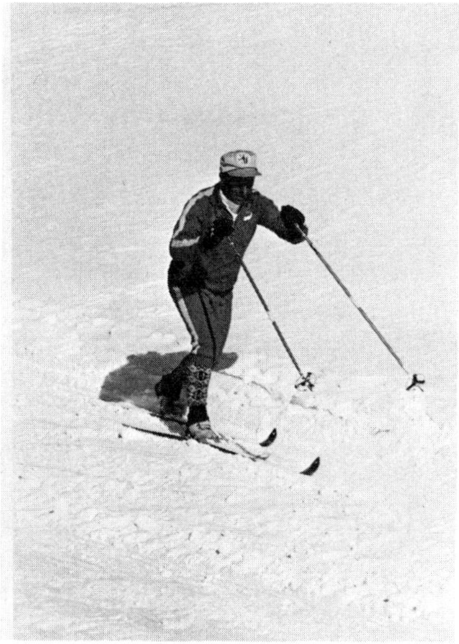
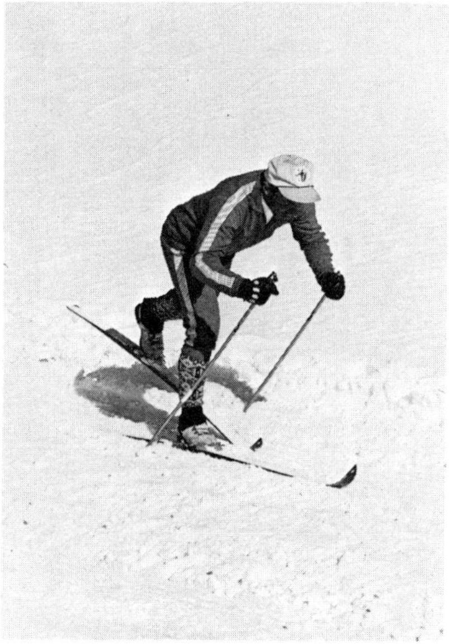
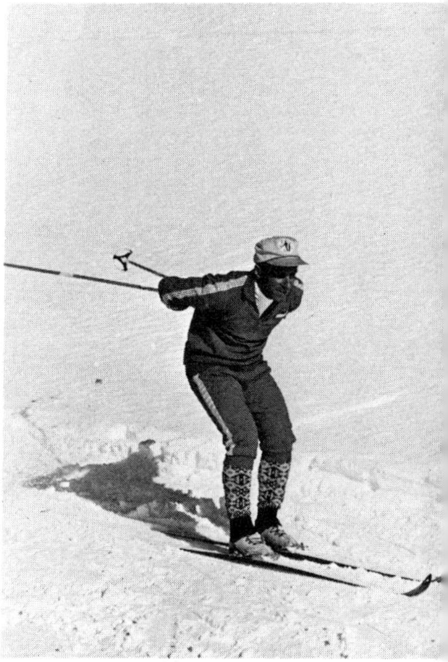

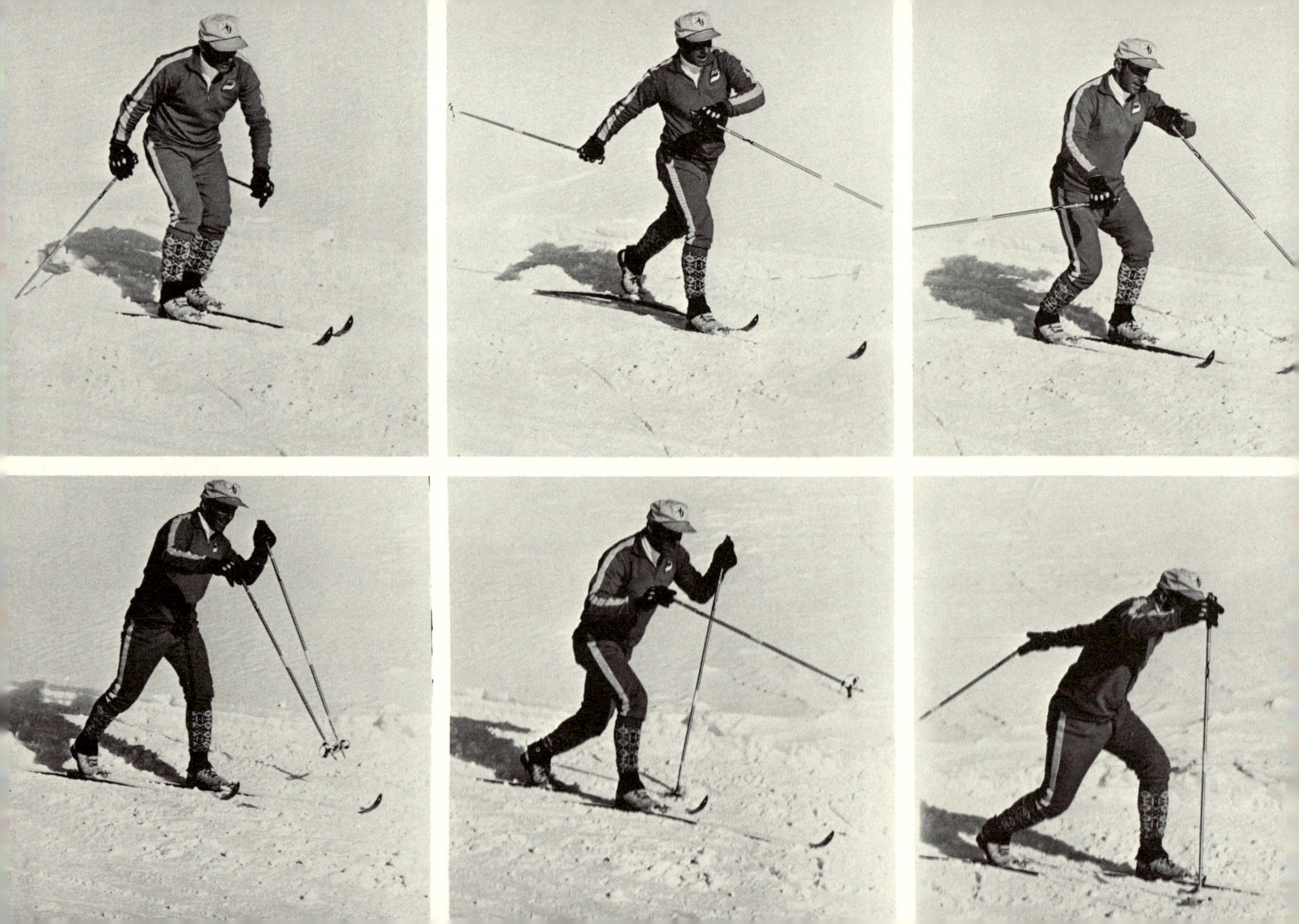

Two-Step Diagonal Poling

Another variation is called two-step diagonal or "change-up" poling. This technique is also known by the unusual name "pole-pole, glide-glide," in an attempt to define exactly what is done — *two* poling motions for every four steps or kicks.

I will put the exercises into four counts, each part representing a kick and a glide. Begin with the regular diagonal poling for the first two strides (strides one and two in the four-count cycle).

The next two strides (three and four) are done at the same speed and same rhythm but without poling. While strides three and four are taking place, the arms are brought forward in a slow, restful motion and replanted in the normal diagonal technique for the next two strides (one and two), which begin the cycle again.

This technique rests the arms and upper body and is useful in terrain where you are getting a good, easy glide.

Combination Poling

A technique utilizing all previously mentioned poling skills (diagonal, double poling and change-up) is called combination poling. You will find that linking the different styles on the trail not only provides variety but is also a very efficient use of touring skills. If the terrain permits, and your legs need a little rest, double-pole without a kick. Or if your arms need a rest, try several kicks and then only one poling motion, as in change-up.

These different techniques are to be used according to terrain. For example, when little glide can be gained, as when climbing a hill, diagonal poling should be used. This can be compared to first gear in an automobile.

On the level with a good glide, changing-up is recommended and is similar to second gear.

With a slight downhill or extremely good glide, all combinations of double poling can be used to achieve the maximum speed from the use of the ski poles. This would be something like third gear.

If the skis are moving at a speed faster than you can kick, then use double poling once in a while, if needed. Otherwise, rest and enjoy the glide. This would be similar to fourth gear.

The diagonal technique combines the stride (sliding the skis over the snow) and poling. By utilizing the various styles of poling and the terrain, the skier becomes freed from man's normal confines and enters the world of gliding motion. Such a skier on a wooded trail or crossing an open field is beautiful to watch: legs and arms working with good extension move him or her along at a nice pace in an easy and graceful manner.

The next skills in the progression are moving step turns, more advanced techniques for moving on the flat. The step turns explained here are an extension of our first exercises, when we turned around the tips and tails of the skis. But now you will move along the prepared track and turn the corners on the move.

Most of the prepared tracks are laid out using a ninety-degree or square corner. Therefore, I suggest two forty-five degree step turns be used to complete the ninety degrees. But if you feel more comfortable taking more steps to round a corner while learning, feel free to do so.

Step Turns on a Corner

There are three ways to do step turns around the tails on corners. The basic differences are the speeds at which they are executed. For practice purposes, use the prepared track with a ninety-degree corner.

Stationary Step Turn: Begin this exercise with your feet at the right-angle corner. A step turn to the left is a four-count exercise.

1) Move the left ski forty-five degrees, or half the turn, and step on it.

2) Bring the right ski alongside the left one.

3) Repeat steps one and two to complete the ninety-degree turn and the four steps.

The turn is started from the prepared track and will end in it at a right angle from where you began.

Moving Step Turn: The same procedure as in the stationary step turn is followed, but this time you add a sliding motion, deep-knee bend and quicker turning steps.

Approach the corner with knees moderately bent, weight on the whole foot. Start the turn just prior to reaching the corner. The steps must be made quickly so that you will finish the turn in the track at a right angle.

stationary step turn

Skate Turn: This turn can be used to increase speed around a corner and is done in the same basic manner as in ice skating. I will explain the skate turn to the left.

As you approach the corner, assume extreme knee bend, weight on both feet, emphasis on the heels.

As you initiate the turn, transfer all your weight to the *right* ski, which is edged to the inside of the turn. Drive or push off this ski forty-five degrees onto the sliding *left* ski and weight it. Bring the right ski alongside, edge it, and repeat the process once more to complete the right-angle turn.

During the execution of the complete skate turn, knees must be well bent at all times, not only for push and drive but also for necessary balance.

You now should be able to ski fairly well around the track. Remember, when touring, the eyes should be focused about fifteen feet to infinity in front of you, not always looking at your skis.

This relaxes the upper body and provides better balance to see and observe the countryside. Relax, eyes off ski tips, and look ahead: three important points on the trail.

As you practice this flatland technique, watch out for common mistakes that plague many beginners. Avoid walking like a woman in a tight skirt; instead, use a long stride. Be careful not to lean too far forward. Keep your hips under you. In a short time, you should see great improvement in your balance and general skiing ability.

2 3

3 Up and Down Hills: Elementary Technique

Where to Practice

A good place to begin hill technique for ski-touring is a small slope with a large flat area at the bottom. You should be able to ski the hill straight without going too fast, and there should be space to coast to a stop on the flat.

A country meadow with a small hill to one side works well for learning climbing skills, and such a spot will get you out in the woods for a short trip. I have known instructors who have used a small hill on the edge of a snow-covered lake, which works nicely. But make sure the ice is a safe thickness!

Knowing technique is important. It is the key to climbing a slope simply and to conserving energy for the remainder of the tour, especially the thrill of skiing down. Going up doesn't have to be a tiring part of ski-touring. Depending on the steepness of a hill, there are five basic techniques to choose from to get to the summit easily.

You should be able to practice all of these climbing techniques on your practice hill. The first uphill skill in the progression is the uphill traverse, which is usually employed when ascending a fairly long, steep, wide hill covered with fresh snow. The same hill with hard-packed snow should probably be climbed with a forward side step.

Walking up a beginner's hill using the diagonal technique is called straight climbing. A vertical side step is used for very steep, narrow places. For similar places where the slope is not quite as steep and the snow a little softer, the herringbone may be used. The herringbone will get you to the top a little faster than a side step, but may be more tiring.

Let's begin with the uphill traverse.

Uphill Traverse

An uphill traverse is nothing more than climbing diagonally across a hill, using the basic touring technique with diagonal poling. Keep a fully weighted ski on the snow for maximum hold from the wax. Leaning too far forward may cause the skis to slip. An erect position above the waist helps place weight squarely over the skis and makes climbing easier.

Approach the hill at a slight angle and begin climbing. (The ski nearest the top of the hill is called the uphill ski. The other is called the downhill ski.) When climbing, take your time. There is no need to rush to the top of the hill, unless you are in a race. As you climb, the surrounding vista will usually improve. Learn to enjoy it.

Climbing should be done in a relaxed manner. If you begin to tire, slow down. If you wander into terrain you don't think you can ski successfully, turn back and choose another route. Be flexible and try to use common sense, whether you are in the hills, mountains, or lowlands.

When you've crossed the hill with an uphill traverse, do a kick turn and traverse the hill in the opposite direction. You should find that the skis stick to the snow if weighted and waxed properly. Wax makes climbing much easier.

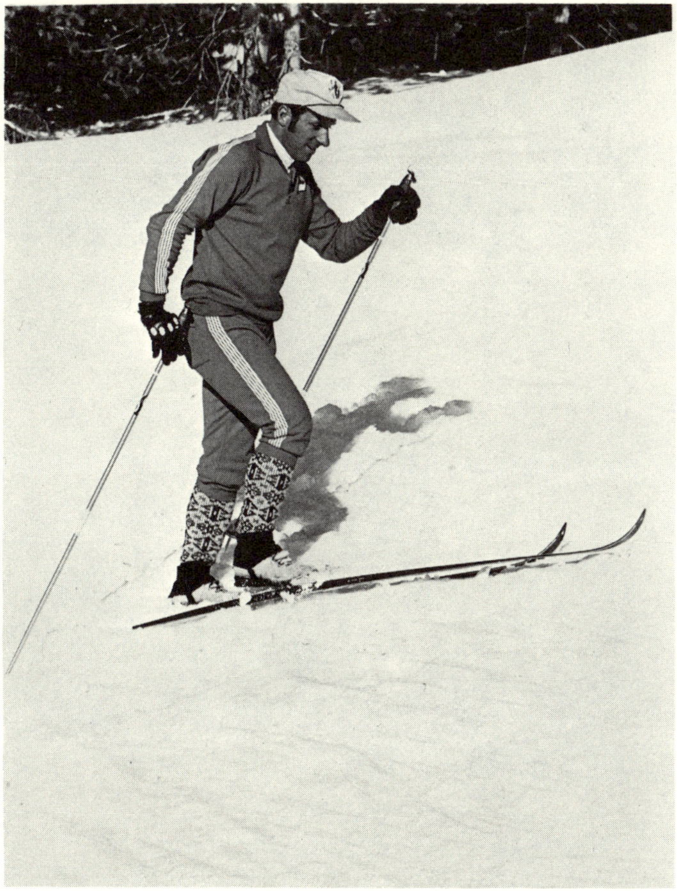

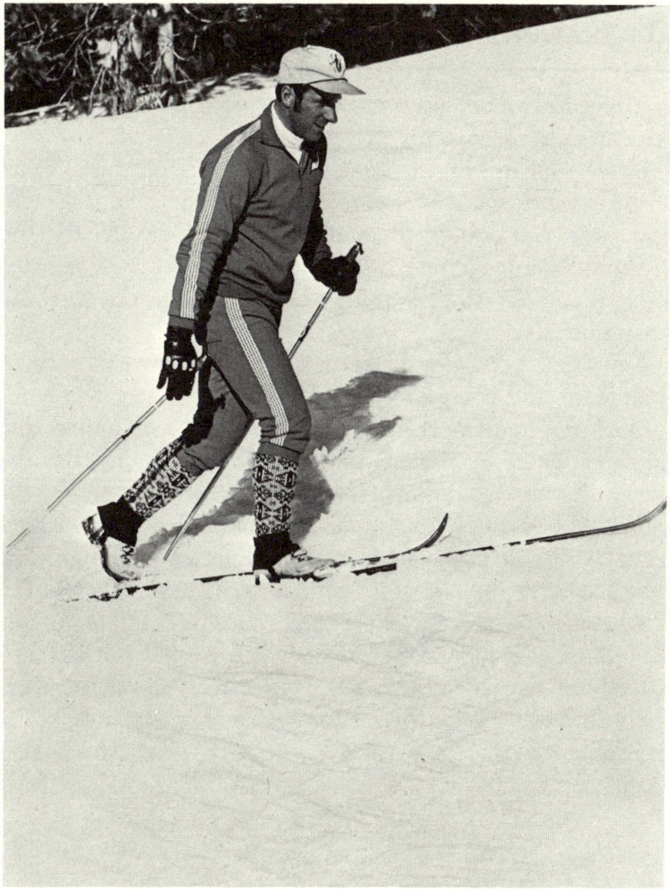

The Forward Side Step

The forward side step is generally used on hard snow or on a steeper slope, where edge set is necessary.

Move your uphill ski about sixteen inches up the hill and at the same time about twelve inches in front of you. Weight and edge (by rolling your ankles slightly toward the top of the hill) it for support. Bring the lower ski up alongside. Weight and edge the downhill ski. Then repeat the climbing procedure.

Each time you move a ski, move a pole. This will become automatic, and poles give added balance.

With the uphill traverse or forward side step, almost any angle of attack may be used, depending on the hold of the wax and your technique. The more vertical the climb, the more hold you need, which is only natural. Going straight up the hill will take you up the fall line, an imaginary line that indicates the steepest, vertical part of the slope.

A vertical climb may take more effort if your technique and wax are not working well. A nice angle of attack is a fifteen to twenty percent grade, crisscrossing the slope, using the uphill traverse or forward side step and kick turns when needed.

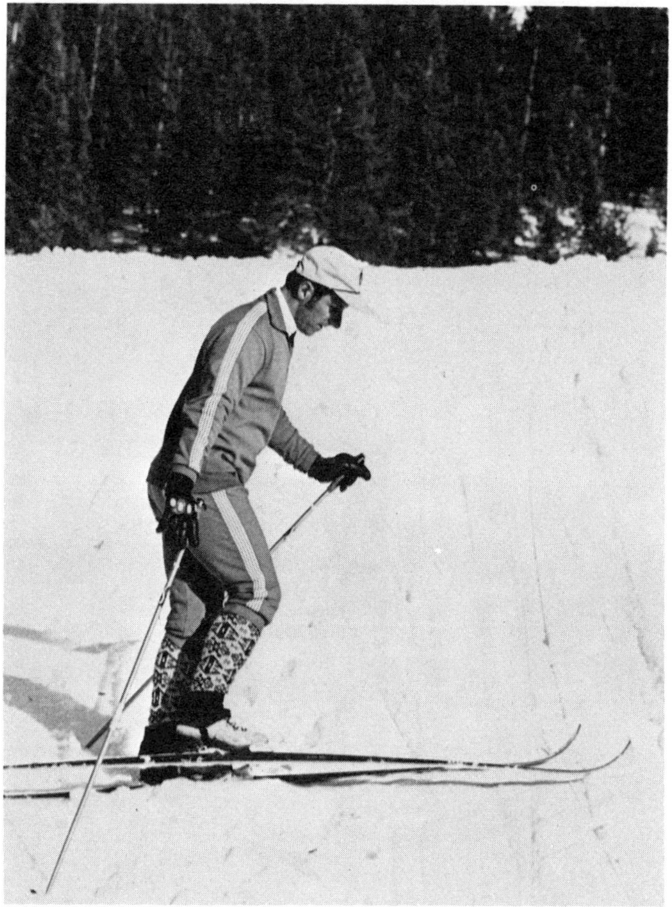

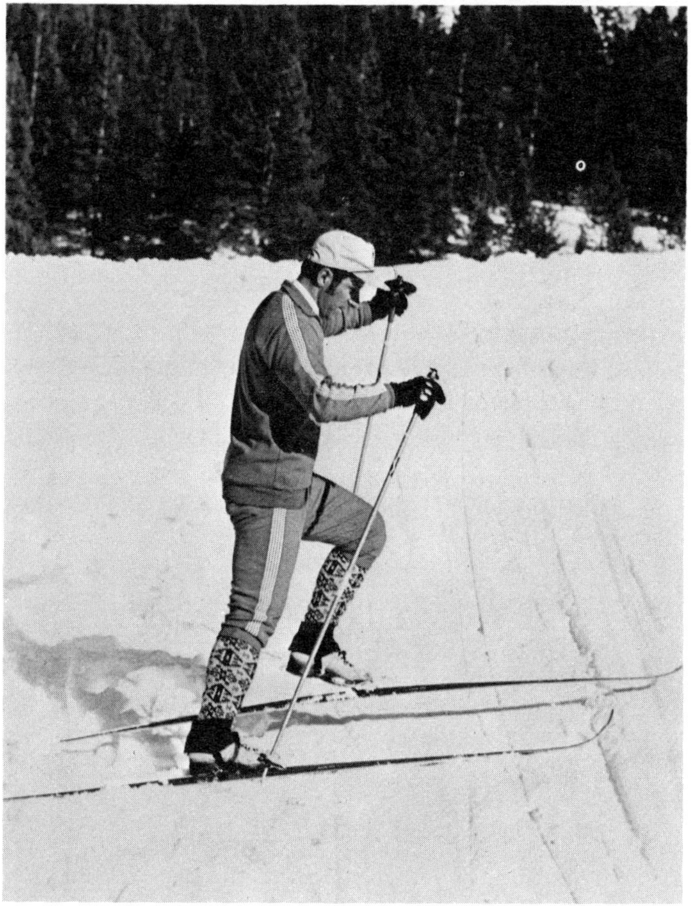

Straight Climbing

Going straight up the fall line, using the diagonal technique, is called "straight climbing." This is one of the easiest ways to reach a summit, especially when conditions are right.

I recommend these suggestions to get maximum hold from your wax:

— Always transfer weight to the forward ski.
— Keep knees bent and back erect, similar to the deep-knee position explained in Chapter 2.
— Keep the hip forward on the weighted ski when climbing.
— A pole should always be behind you in the pole-check position to prevent a slide backwards if the wax breaks loose.

Now climb a small hill, using the straight-climb method. A common mistake with beginners is to lean too far forward. This may cause the wax to break loose and could result in a fall. Remember to slap the skis on the snow if more hold is needed from the wax.

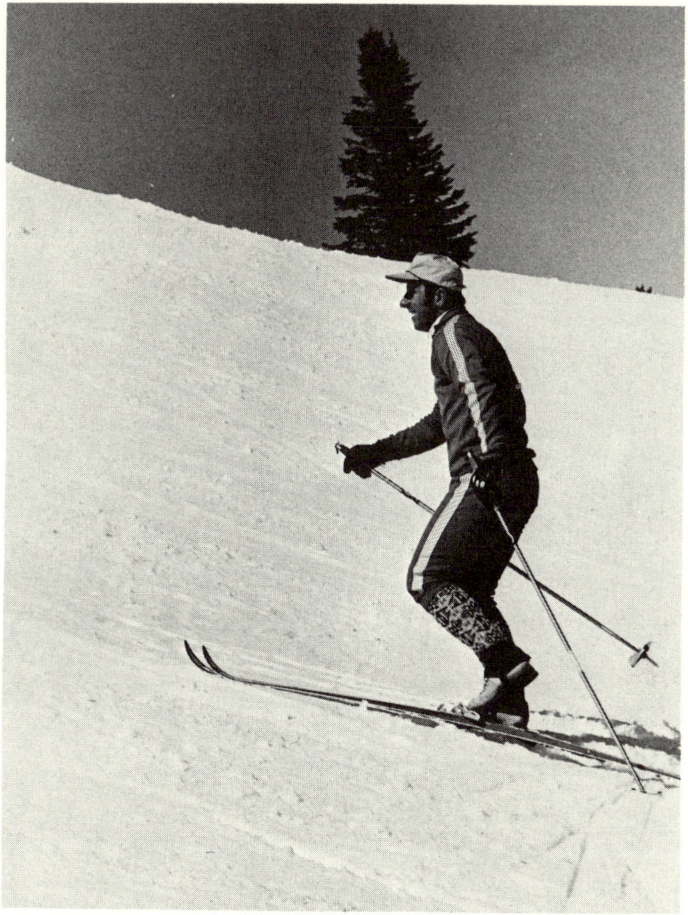
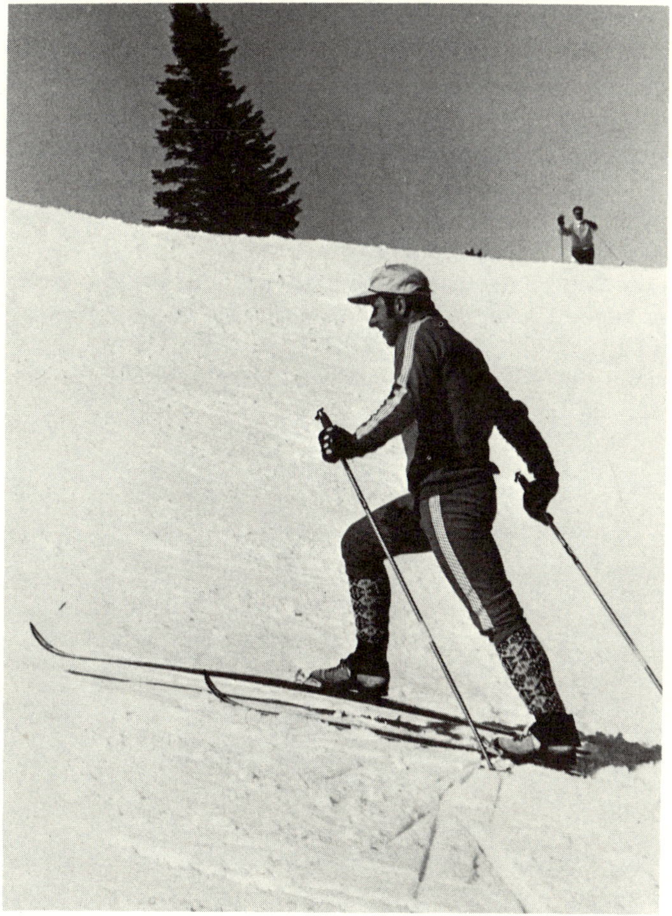

The Vertical Side Step

The vertical side step should be used for climbing very steep slopes. Stand across the fall line, skis parallel and edged, pointed neither uphill nor downhill. Move the uphill ski and pole about a foot up the slope and set the edge. Bring the other ski and pole alongside that ski.

For better edge control on a steeper hill, you can stamp the edge of your ski into the snow. This is called "setting an edge."

Sometimes, another climbing technique, called the herringbone, may be used to scale a hill.

Herringbone

Begin the herringbone at the bottom of the hill. Place your skis in a "V" position, tips apart and tails nearly joined. With weight on the whole foot and ankles turned in slightly, edging the skis, walk up the slope, moving first one ski and then the other. Poles should be to the side and slightly behind you. Your hands may be placed over the tops of the poles for support and assistance in climbing.

You must maintain the "V" position or you will have a tendency to slide backwards. If needed, you may slap the skis down for more hold.

In addition to wax, there are other devices that hold a ski on the snow when climbing. They are called "climbers," or "skins," and are attached to the running surface of the ski. Skins (named because some are made from sealskin) have short hair that sticks into the snow when climbing and does a good job of holding the skis. When moving forward, the bristles, or hair, lie flat, allowing the skis to slide.

In addition to sealskins, climbers can be made of mohair, canvas, plastic, and other materials. In some special conditions, skins may be extremely useful. For example, ski mountaineers will use them when climbing several miles, especially when they don't have to continually put them on and take them off, and when they are wearing heavy backpacks. But with today's modern ski-base materials and waxes, skins have little practical value for the normal tour over rolling terrain.

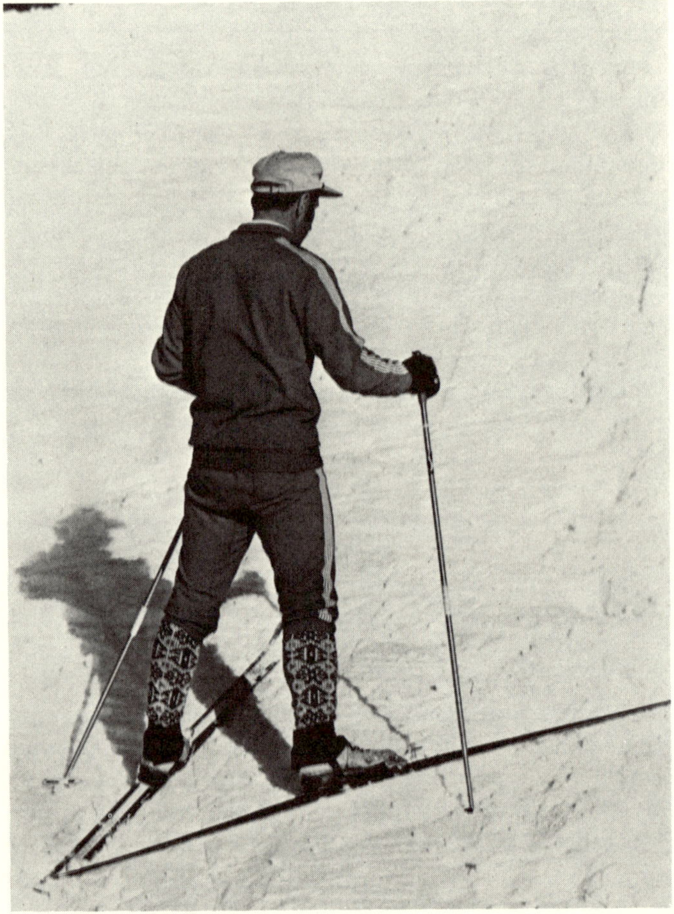

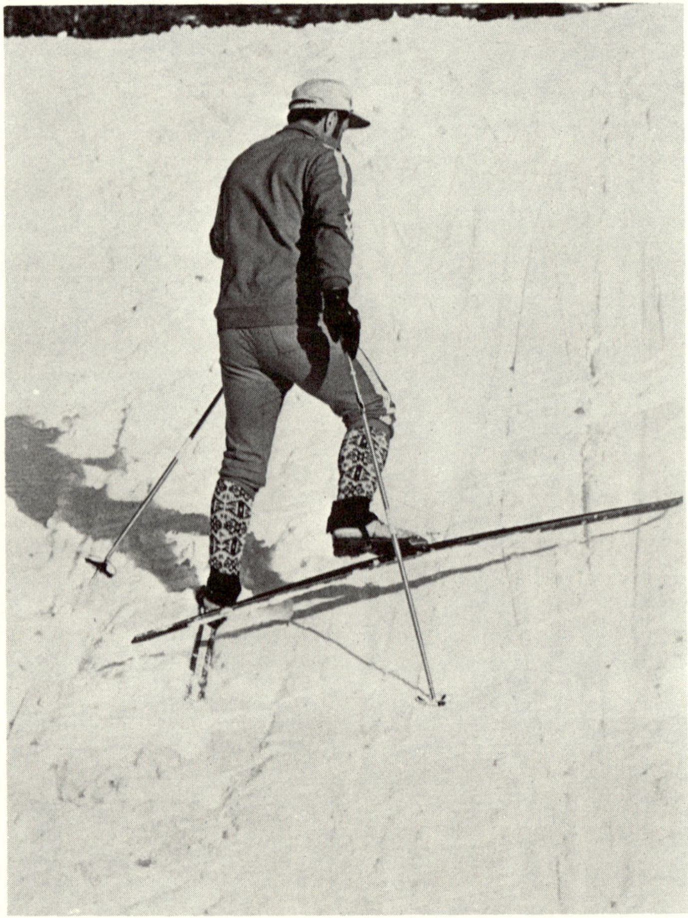

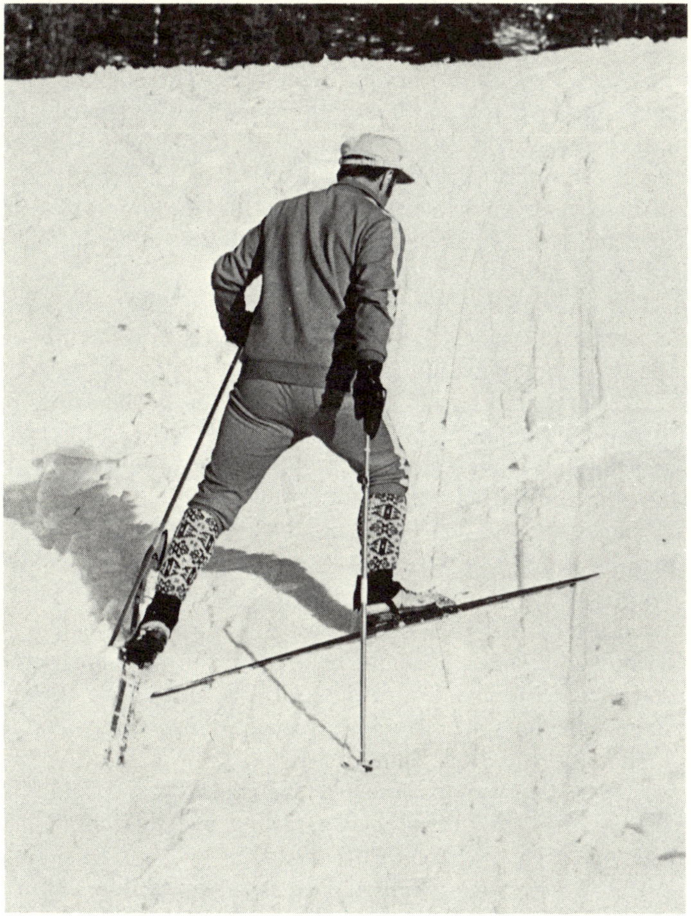
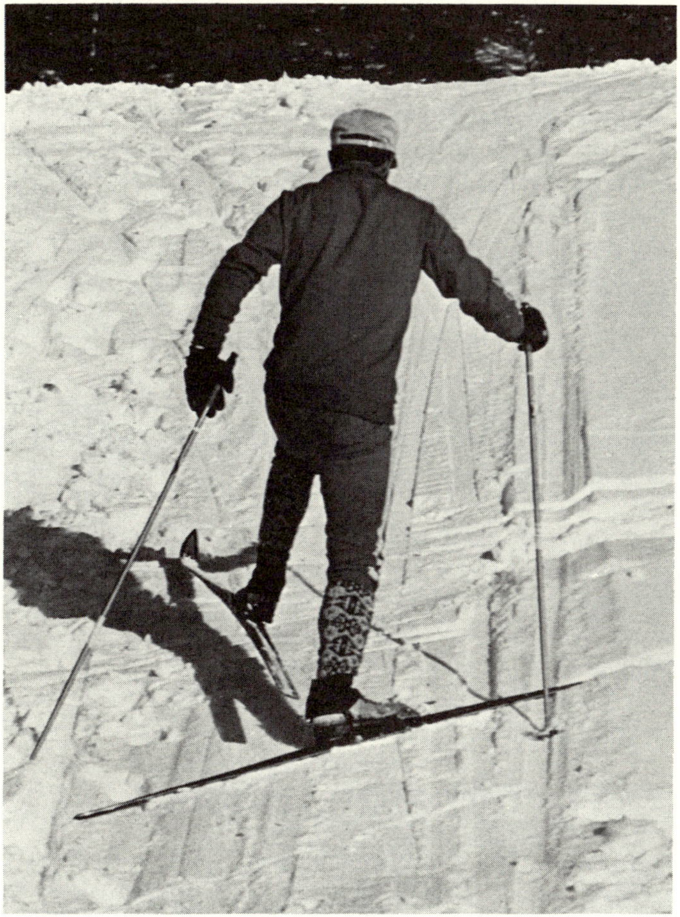

In the days before ski lifts, when the touring binding was common, gunnysacks were used as climbers to assist in getting to the top of the hills. Then ski lifts arrived, along with the push-button world, and the touring attachment to an Alpine ski vanished almost like the buggy whip.

It was a natural transition to make. People who worked hard physically all week didn't want to climb hills with downhill skis on weekends. They wanted ski lifts to carry them up. But today, the work week is more mentally than physically fatiguing, and the urge to use the body in a relaxing physical way is becoming stronger. People want to get away from the hassle of congestion, noise and pressure and into a quiet, toned-down atmosphere.

The winter wilderness provides an outlet for these individuals. Not machine- or noise-oriented, they want to ski slowly into the woods and be part of that life — even if it's only for a short time.

The woods and mountains of this country should be used. There should be places preserved for the quiet life. Ski-touring, modernized by lightweight equipment and other advantages of technology, will let you utilize the winter wilderness without leaving a scar.

Whatever the reasons for the increased popularity in ski-touring, and I suppose they are as many as there are skiers, the old style of cross-country, still in existence, is giving way to newer concepts and newer equipment.

After practicing the climbing techniques, you should be ready for a little downhill skiing. The practice slope you have chosen should be gentle enough to ski straight. The area should have plenty of room at the bottom to coast to a stop.

Skiing downhill is a unique experience. The downhill run immediately takes you away from your normal pace and into a new world of motion, even if you ski slowly. The world's record for speed on skis is well over a hundred miles an hour. You might start by going three or four miles an hour and when you become confident, twenty miles an hour will seem easy.

The thrill of descent, the sensation of sliding over snow, enhances ski-touring. Let me tell you a true story before we begin learning downhill technique.

In the winter of 1970 an older woman from the southern part of the United States took ski lessons from me. Touring was the first winter activity she had tried; in fact, she had never seen snow before coming to Colorado that winter.

She was naturally curious and progressed well in class. But she wasn't to the point of taking a downhill run before her group had to leave the mountains.

During her last time out, she asked me what it was like to ski downhill, and if I could help her down a gentle slope. We climbed to the top of a small hill, and as we started down, I held her arm to keep her from falling.

The ride was slow, but long and smooth. When the run was over, the woman turned to me excitedly and said, "In all my years, I've never had a feeling like that! That has been one of the greatest thrills of my life!"

The woman was delighted, and she taught me a lesson I

won't forget. Long ago, I had forgotten the excitement of skiing down a small hill. It was something that vanished with so many years of skiing since childhood. But this woman brought back those young memories and taught me to realize what my students must be experiencing — the thrill of descent. Now I share that delight with them.

Downhill: Straight Running Position

The position used to ski downhill is very logical. Skis are parallel, four to six inches apart; ankles and knees are slightly bent forward; the upper body is erect from the hips, arms hanging loosely, hands about hip-high. You must be relaxed.

Weight should be equally distributed on both skis, one ski slightly forward for stability.

Stand on your skis and move your body back and forth until you find a position that feels "secure" to you. Generally, that will be the balance point. Look ahead a few yards. Free your skis from the snow by sliding them back and forth before pushing off. Now, give it a go!

You might find yourself weaving around as you ski down, trying to keep your balance. This is normal. Look ahead for terrain changes, especially the transition from the hill to the flat.

Each time you ski down, you should feel more confident. Practice shifting your weight from one ski to another, bending your knees, and coasting on one ski at a time. These exercises will help you get the "feel" of sliding on snow.

Falling

As long as you ski, and regardless of how well you do it, I guarantee you will take a few spills now and then. Everyone does. It's part of the sport.

During a fall, remember to stretch out, and try to relax. (The first photograph illustrates the correct way to fall.) You want to achieve a slide with a fully extended body and to avoid tucking (the second photograph), which is apt to cause a knee or elbow to catch in the snow, sending you tumbling or rolling. Try not to tighten up. Relax as you slide.

The Telemark Position

A straight running position that may be used when greater balance and stability are needed, especially over bumpy terrain, is the telemark position. This position is different from the telemark turn, which has become synonymous with old-style skiing. Advanced touring skiers still use the traditional telemark turn, but now mostly for exhibition and fun.

The telemark position can be described as half a genuflection, or a partial bending of the knees to the ground, one foot back, weight evenly distributed. Assume a downhill position. Move a ski forward until one tip is about eighteen inches ahead of the other. Drop *straight* down, bending both knees — not your back. The front knee should be well forward, body erect from the waist up.

The telemark may be used when skiing downhill to regain balance when necessary. For example, when you are skiing down a hill in a straight running position and see a patch of ice or a snow drift ahead, use a telemark for added stability in these more difficult situations. Don't forget to use your leg muscles to retain balance.

Practice going from a straight running position into a telemark, an exercise that improves balance and gives you a sense of security.

The next skills to learn are turns. Touring skiers use many Alpine turns. Basic skills include step turns, skate turns, step turns traversing a hill, snowplow turns and stem turns. The stem christie, christie and parallel turns are for more advanced students. (See Chapter 6.)

Most Alpine turns can be done on touring skis with slight modification. The touring skier must compensate for not having his heel locked to the ski, an integral part of Alpine skiing. Therefore, touring skiers must remember to always keep *some* weight on the heel of the foot during most downhill turns. Having weight on the whole foot is important.

Sometimes I am asked why the heel isn't locked to the ski when skiing downhill. That would be a step backward to the days before release bindings. Those who remember the "bear trap" bindings (that locked the boot firmly to the ski) know how dangerous they were.

I won't allow any fixed-heel bindings on my tours, purely for safety reasons. The ski patrol isn't in the backcountry or scattered throughout the woods. Why ask for trouble when it isn't necessary?

Other differences between touring and Alpine turns arise from the design of the skis. The touring ski is narrow, limber, and turns easily in soft, light snow conditions. It is an excellent powder ski. The Alpine ski is stiffer, wider and heavier.

Step Turn onto the Flat

Practicing step turns onto the flat after descending a hill teaches you to turn while moving. The exercise is an extension of the step turns described in Chapter 2.

When doing moving step turns it is only necessary to lift the tip of the ski high enough to make the turn. If the tail of the ski remains on the snow, your balance can be increased.

Points to remember when you reach the flat are:

— Bend your knees more than normally.
— Make sure your weight is on the whole foot, with emphasis on the heel.
— Shift your weight to the right ski (for a left turn) so that you can step to the left with the unweighted ski. Then weight the left ski and bring the other alongside.

By repeating the stepping motion with larger steps and in quick succession, a sharper turn can be made. Practice these moving step turns around the tails in both directions, and then add step turns around tips, moving the *tails* out to change direction.

A step turn around tails will maintain speed while a step-turn around tips will tend to slow you down.

You can see that skills are being used over and over to form a complete touring technique. The step turn is an excellent example of this, demonstrating how the progression is starting to build: the basic step turn on the flat being worked into a moving step turn and then into a step turn from a hill onto the flat.

Skate Turn onto the Flat

Practicing the skate turn onto the flat marks the beginning of edge control, and learning to handle the edges of your skis is important for most downhill techniques.

I have already made the distinction on the slope between the uphill ski and the downhill ski. Each ski also has an inside edge and an outside edge, corresponding to the inside and the outside of the turn. When you are standing across a slope, they are called uphill and downhill edges.

You will see the value of edge control when you push in a new direction with a skate turn onto the flat. The exercise is similar to the previous one with these additions: control the use of your edges with a skating or pushing motion on both skis. As an option, also use both poles to push with.

NOTE: As you make a left turn, you will make a complete weight shift from the right ski to the left. During this time you should use the inside edge of the right ski.

Step Turn from a Downhill Traverse

The next step turn is practiced from a downhill traverse, which simply means skiing across the hill bending your knees, the uphill ski slightly ahead to prevent the tips from crossing. There is one important aspect to the traverse position: you should ride your skis on the *uphill* edges to keep from sliding down the hill sideways. Most of the weight should be on the *downhill* ski. Practice skiing the downhill traverse until you feel fairly comfortable.

Now, as you traverse the slope, with all your weight on the downhill ski, lift the uphill ski, point the tip slightly uphill, and then transfer all your weight to it. Bring the other ski alongside. Several uphill step turns should be made in succession, which will help you control your speed and can bring you to a complete stop.

Using edges and controlling speed are very important. Here is a practice exercise from a downhill traverse: Take two small steps down the slope and then two steps up. You will notice control of direction and speed.

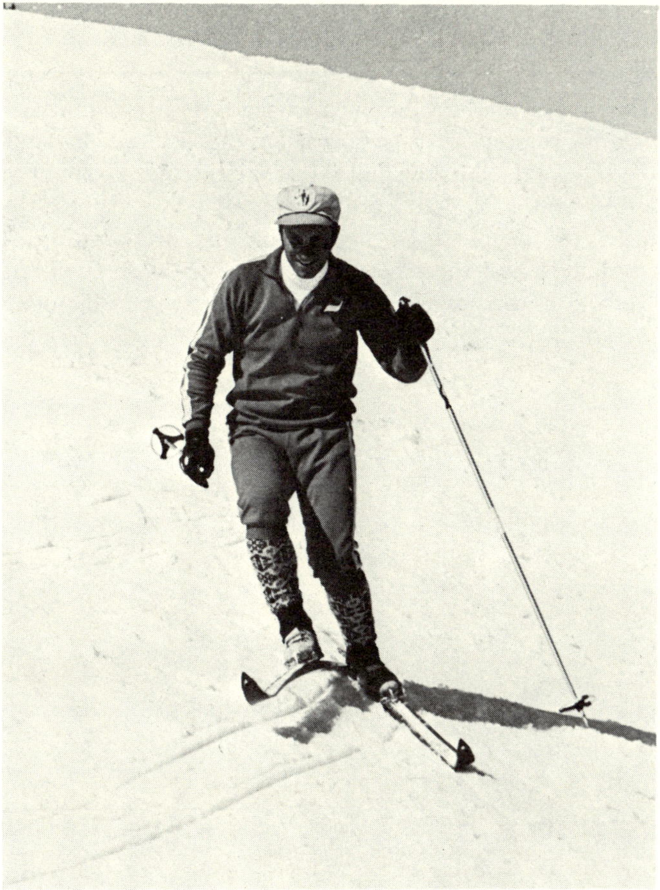

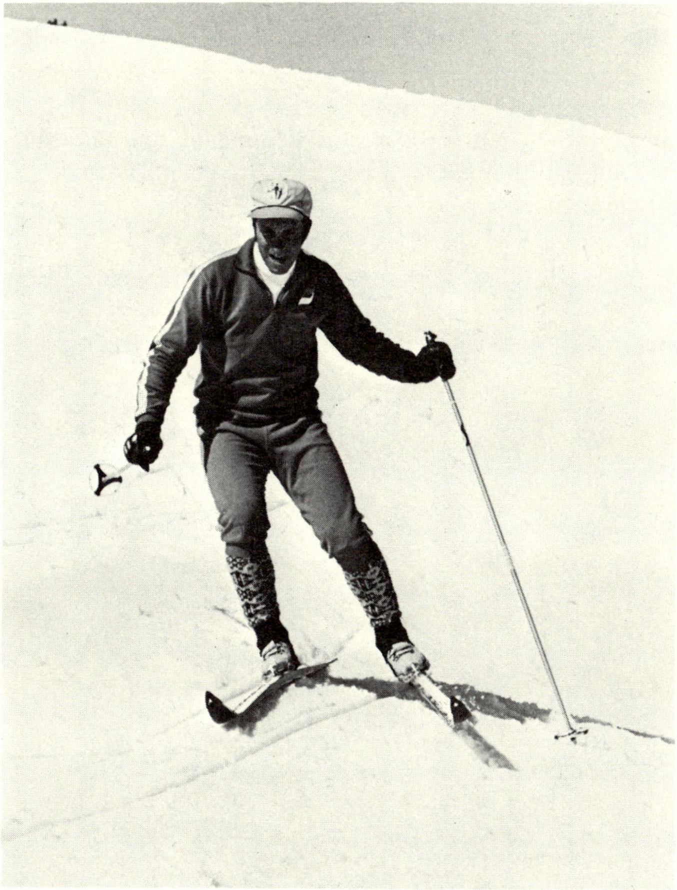

Step Turn from the Fall Line

In a straight running position down the fall line, begin a step turn to the left and continue stepping around until the skis are heading uphill and you come to a stop. Practice in both directions.

This was one of the first ways skiers learned to stop and was part of the Norwegian technique taken to central Europe.

Step Turn around Tips from a Traverse

This technique enables you to make a step turn downhill to control your speed or to slow you down. From a downhill traverse, weight the downhill ski. Move the uphill ski out so the tips are together and the tails apart. Using slight edge, transfer the weight to the uphill ski and bring the other alongside. Repeat the process until you have turned and are traversing in the opposite direction. Now try it in the other direction.

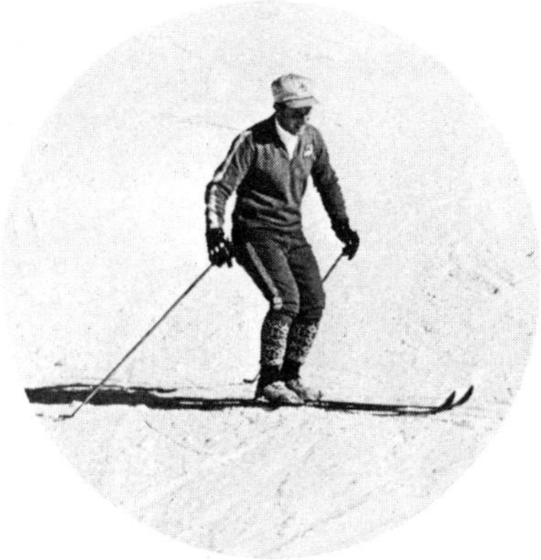
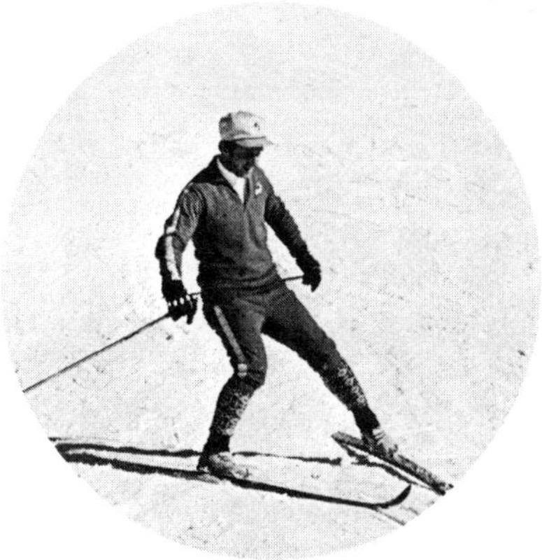
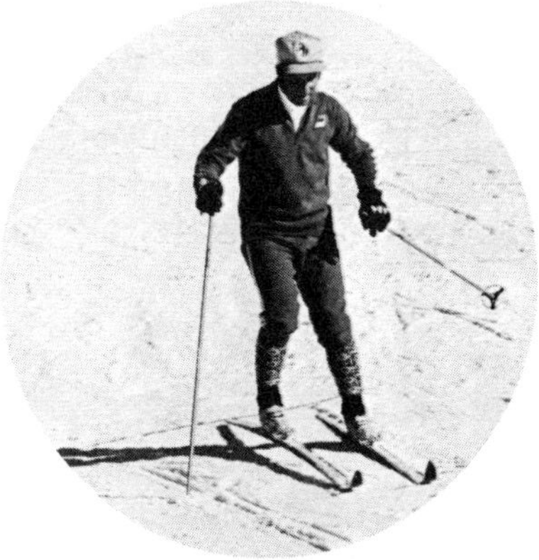
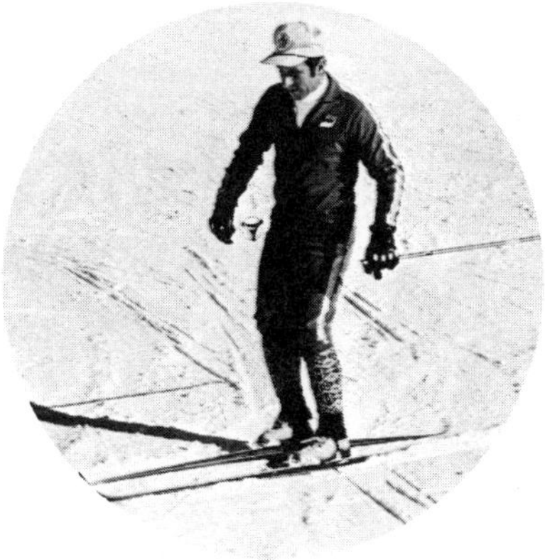
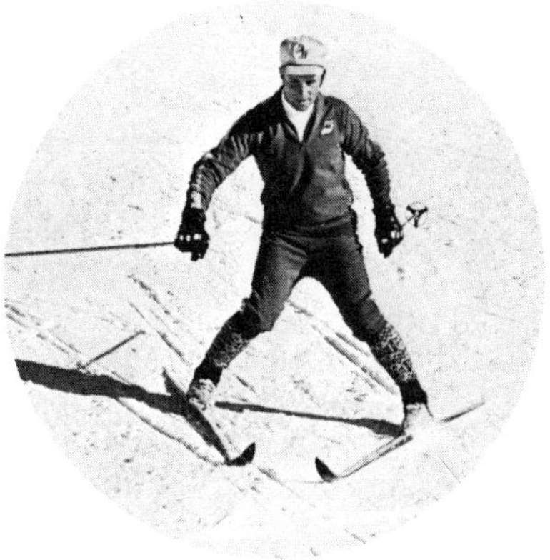

Snowplow Position

Another way to stop and to control speed is the snowplow. Standing on a level area, place the ski tips four to six inches apart, tails widely separated. Bend ankles and knees slightly forward. Arms should be loose. Have definite weight on the heel of your foot, body relaxed. The skis should be in a plow or inverted "V" position.

Snowplow Exercise: Standing with skis together on level ground, jump into a snowplow position and back again several times. This will help prepare you to go into a snowplow while moving.

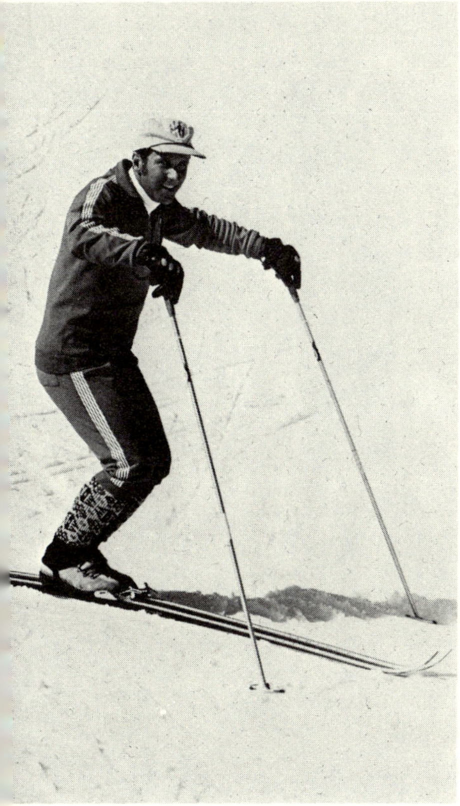
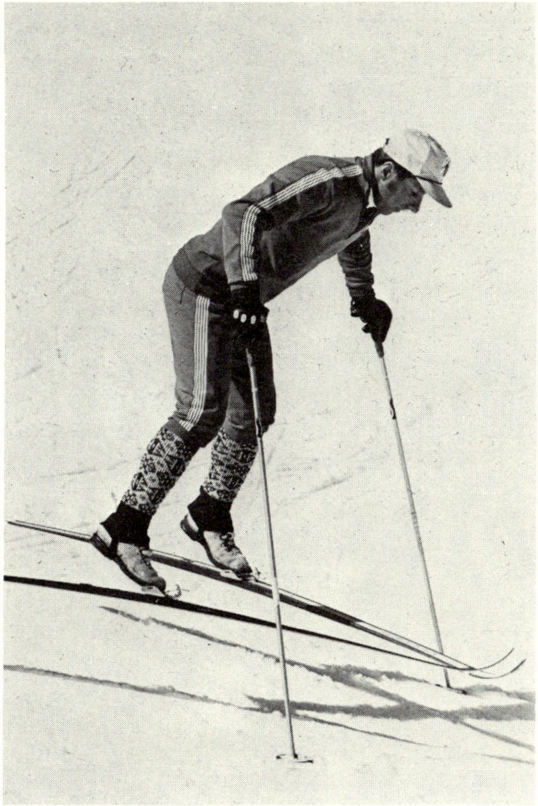
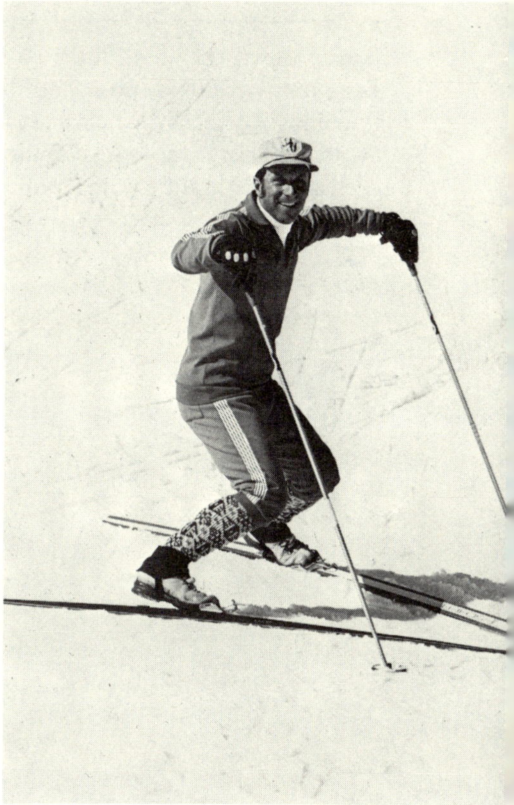

The Snowplow

Coast down the small hill in a straight running position. About halfway down, push both heels out and move into a snowplow. Keep the tips close enough so you won't take off downhill like a wide-track Pontiac! Lateral foot control is necessary to hold the ski tips in the correct position.

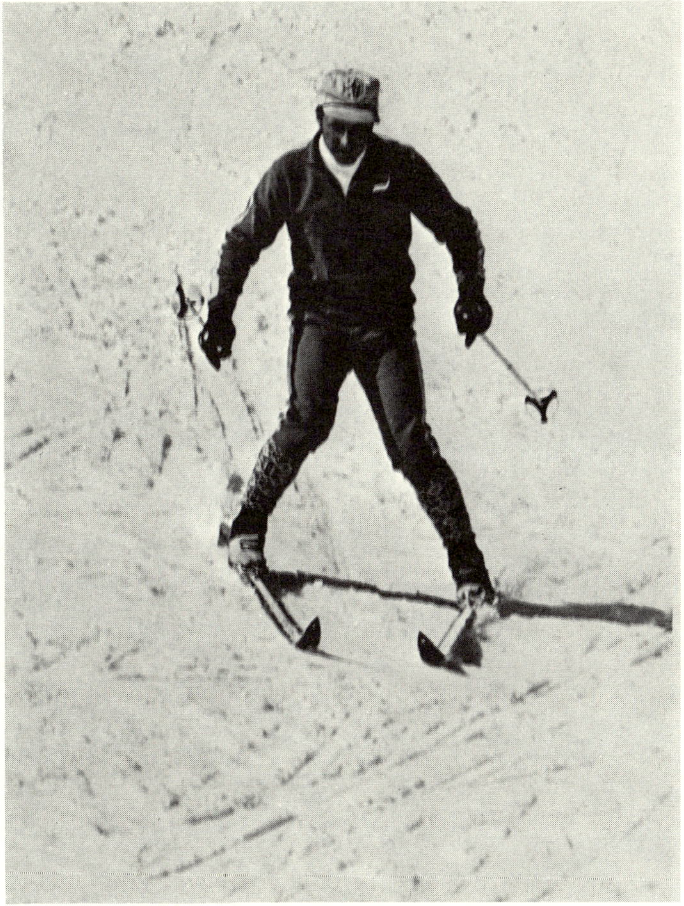

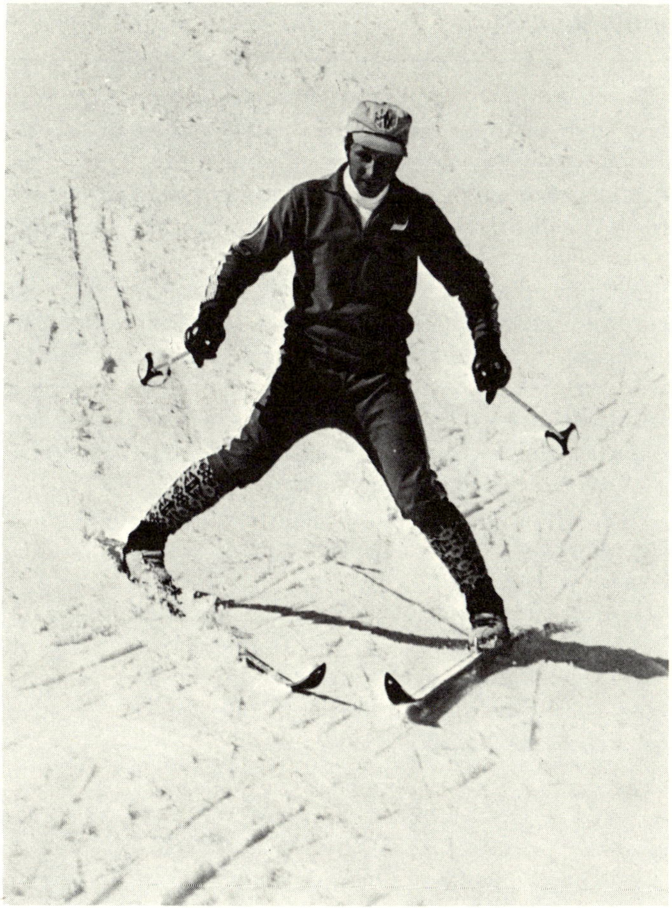

Snowplow Stop

If you keep a wide snowplow position and turn your knees and ankles in, causing the running surface of the skis to move onto their inside edges, you will create a braking effect and soon come to a stop. This technique, used to check speed, is called a snowplow stop. Ankle control is essential to enable you to use the inside edges.

Using a snowplow at high speeds on a steep hill may cause you plenty of trouble, almost guaranteeing a fall. The snowplow should not be used as a high-speed stop. I recommend using the snowplow, snowplow stop or snowplow turns only on a well-packed or hard-snow base. Trying any of the snowplows in breakable crust or rotten snow isn't practical and can cause many falls.

The exercise starts with a straight running position. Do a snowplow. Go back to a straight running position and then use a snowplow stop.

Here is a hint that may save you a lot of trouble while learning these exercises. If you must stop in a hurry, sit down. I don't advocate this except in extreme cases, such as being out of control and heading for a road, tree or other obstacle. Always try to ski under control.

The Pole Drag

There are other ways to slow yourself down. A pole drag, for example, can be used. Take the pole straps off your wrists and place the poles together and to the rear between your legs. Place one hand below the middle of the poles and the other above center. When coming down a hill, apply drag on the snow by pressing on the ski poles. You can even use body weight to help create the necessary drag.

This skill may be used with a snowplow for added braking power. It is a good way to keep your speed down, especially on a narrow, winding trail.

The pole drag may also be used to either side of the skier instead of between the legs, but it is usually not as effective. Removing pole straps from wrists is important, for if the strap is on and the pole gets caught on a bush or branch, you could injure your arm. If a pole gets tangled, let it go and retrieve it later. The same principle applies when downhill skiing through the trees.

The Snowplow Turn

Ski down the fall line in a snowplow, skis edged to the inside and equally weighted. Shift your weight to one ski and bend that knee and ankle forward. Remember to keep weight on your heels.

To make a *left* turn, weight the *right* ski. You should have the downhill (right) ski edged in to make the turn. Practice snowplow turns in both directions.

Linked Snowplow Turns

To begin, start at the top of the hill. Ski down the fall line in a snowplow, skis slightly edged. Shift your weight to one ski. As you begin to make a turn, shift your weight to the opposite ski to change direction. By weighting one ski and then another, successive turns to the right and left can be made.

Besides weight shift, linked snowplow turns can be made by twisting the upper body, sometimes called "rotation." For example, when a turn to the right is initiated, the upper body should begin to rotate to the right, or clockwise. For a left turn, the body should begin to rotate to the left, or counterclockwise.

The Stem Turn

A more advanced turn, and the next in the progression, is the stem turn. Start in a downhill traverse, weight on the downhill ski; let's say the left ski, for explanation purposes.

Slide the uphill ski (the right one) into a stem, which is nothing more than a snowplow position.

Transfer your weight to the right ski, which is edged slightly, helping to initiate the turn. As the turn is completed, the right ski will become the downhill ski and should receive most of the weight.

The left ski should slide parallel to the right to form a new downhill traverse. Now you will be headed in the opposite direction from which you started.

This is living: skiing downhill in control, being able to turn and stop.

By now you should have learned the basic technique that will help you ski successfully over almost any normal touring terrain.

These are the basics of ski-touring, but there are many other refinements to know, such as clothing, equipment, waxing, selecting terrain, snow safety and more advanced turns, including those for deep-powder skiing.

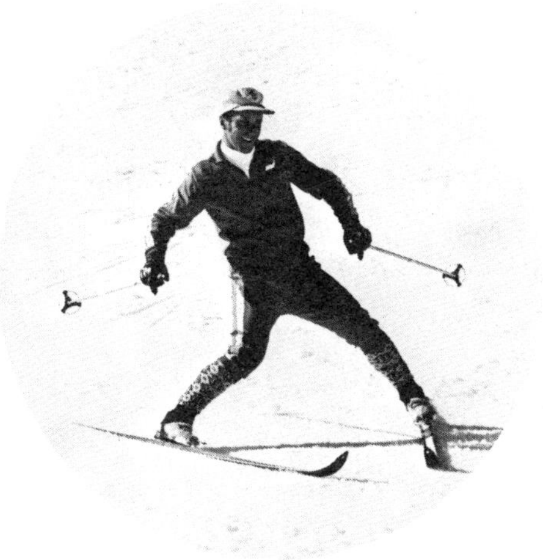
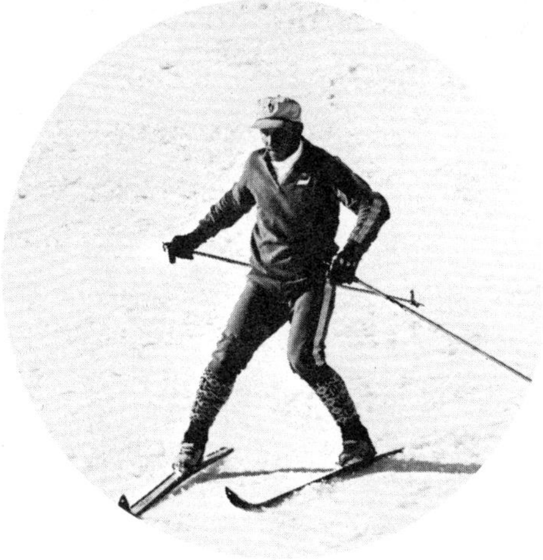
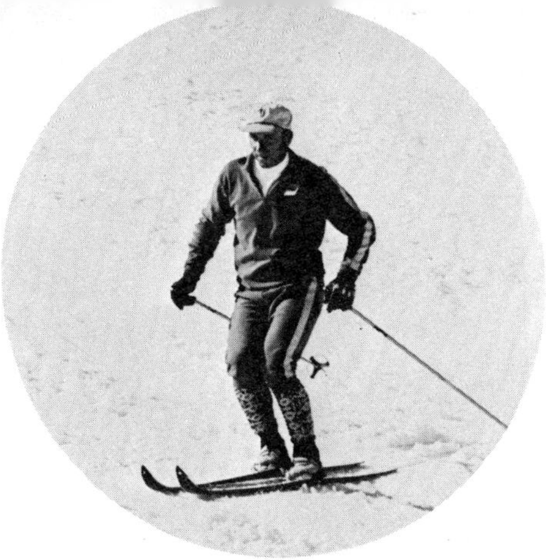
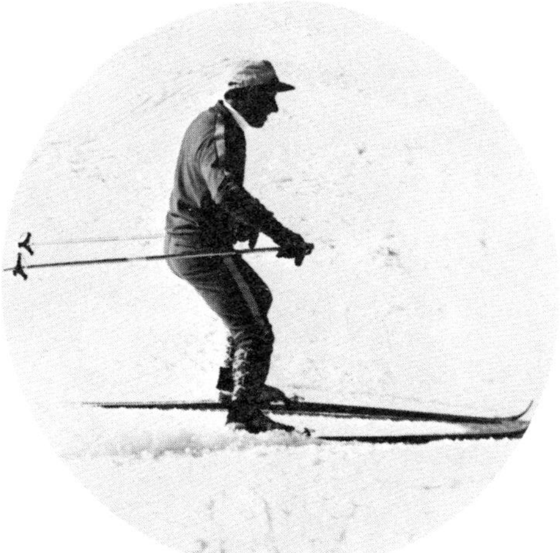
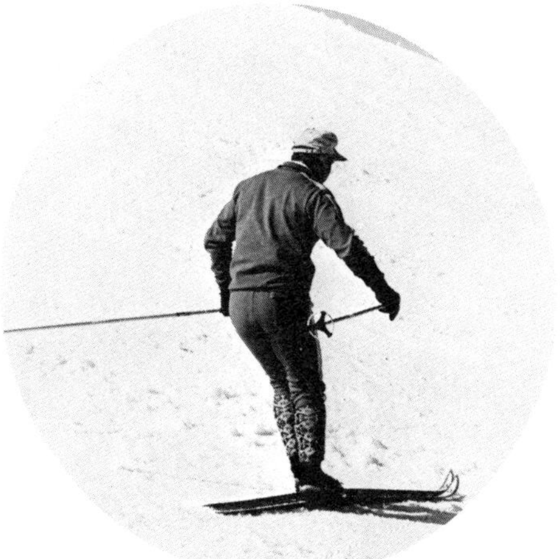

4 | Day Touring: Planning and Preparation

Introduction

Once you have learned the basic touring techniques, you are ready to travel on a day tour with confidence. The success of your tour will rely not only on technique but also on planning and preparation.

Ski-touring enthusiasts usually have a desire for exploring and adventure, a nagging urge to see the other side of the mountain. This is the way the sport should be and is a big part of touring enjoyment.

But if a trip is disorganized, skiers may become soured on the sport for good. More than one beginner has told me he had been "taken" on his first tour. Their stories usually contain several ingredients. It was the skier's first time, he went too far, climbed too much, was asked to ski down a steep slope, or used the wrong wax. This produced exhaustion and fear. When the tour was over, the first-timer was tired and sore and convinced touring is something that belongs to cross-country ski racers.

Advanced terrain is for advanced skiers. They have a great time skiing such a route. However, the beginner doesn't belong on an expert's journey. A less experienced skier shouldn't be forced to keep up. A tour should be led with the slowest person in mind, and then everyone will have a good time. The beginner will want to go again, and the expert will look forward to more of a challenge on advanced terrain.

A Touring Group

Touring groups can be a mixed bag of experiences and ages — variety is the spice of life. A trip with children, teen-agers, and adults probably should be short and easy, taking into account each person's ability. An adult who has a sedentary job during the week might want to take an easier tour than a more active individual.

If there are strong and weak skiers in a party, you might want to divide the tour in two. Every group, however, should be made up of at least four persons (for safety reasons) and not more than ten per instructor or leader.

Why at least four? In case of injury or equipment failure, one skier can stay with the person in trouble and two can go for help, so one person is never left alone in the backcountry or woods. This is known as the buddy system.

Never leave a skier by himself, whether he is in difficulty or not. This is a cardinal rule of the sport!

The Leader

Touring is enjoyed best when the group is nearly equal in ability, except for the leader. He is generally the one person in the group considered the best all-around skier and outdoorsman. Beginning groups should have a good instructor-leader.

The leader is responsible for each member's welfare. He sets the pace, which is about one mile an hour for beginning skiers. Remember, the sport isn't a race. Take your time and enjoy yourself.

On a beginning tour, it is nice to have an experienced skier in the rear to assist newer members. Those who have toured before probably know a few hints to make a trip easier.

The person in charge should have the knowledge to choose the route and the length of the tour. He may make the journey long or short depending on his judgment of weather, terrain and skier ability. He should make sure there are rest stops and always be on the lookout for equipment failure. A good touring instructor can make the difference between a safe, enjoyable trip and an exhausting workout. I recommend that potential leaders keep a good sense of humor, and patience is a must!

Route Selection

Beginners should start with a nice, easy trip over gently rolling terrain. The tour should be planned so that you are never more than a half-mile from a road, farmhouse, or cabin. The better skier and outdoorsman you become, the longer trips you can take with confidence.

The makeup of the group will determine how much up and down it can handle. Obviously, it will be harder for young children to make a long climb. If you are going to make a one-way tour, you should plan for transportation. "Out-and-returns" won't require shuttling cars or having somebody meet the group at the end of the trip.

Snow Conditions and Avalanches

Snow conditions will play a major part in route selection. Snow is an amazingly changeable substance. It can be fluffy or hard, dry or wet, crusty or slushy, and is continually changing or moving. Snow knowledge is essential for extensive travel in the backcountry, and it may help you avoid an avalanche.

Snowslides can descend with the full force of a tidal wave or they can whisper over the frozen earth. Either way, avalanches are full of unexpected fury and danger, and so some knowledge of avalanche signs is important.

To become an avalanche expert takes a lot of time and study, but there are some practical guidelines that are helpful in the backcountry. Try to get the latest snow report before starting your trip. The Forest Service and outdoor information centers should have good predictions of possible slide areas. Stay away from them. Be aware of natural warning systems, such as other slide areas and drumming (when a large snow field settles all at once, making a noise). Both are signs of unstable snow conditions.

Here is some general information condensed from the federal government's *Snow-Survey Safety Guide*.

Slides are apt to occur on slopes steeper than twenty-five degrees, with the critical zone at thirty-five degrees or more. Other prime snowslide conditions include fair weather and rapidly rising temperatures after a heavy storm; and in the spring, above-freezing temperatures for thirty-six hours, which promote deep thawing and wet slides. Rain has the same effect.

Steep, untimbered gullies are natural slide paths, as are steep scars on timbered slopes. Heavily wooded hillsides are less apt to slide. Steep southerly slopes favor avalanches in new snow and in late spring. Deep thawing of snow fields on steep, open slopes is dangerous.

Avalanche danger is greatest after at least ten inches of snow have fallen and for the twenty-four to forty-eight hours following such a storm. There are several signs of avalanche danger:

— An overhanging cornice (pile of snow on a leeward ridge created by blowing wind) that may break away and cause the snow on the slope beneath to slide.
— Dry snow underfoot that is soft, deep and doesn't pack into a clean, sharp track.
— Damp snow that slithers out from underfoot and rolls away in balls or slips away like a blanket.
— Sun-formed snowballs.
— Wind-packed slab snow on steep slopes (this snow settles suddenly underfoot with a crunching sound and may fracture into blocks and start an avalanche).

When ski-touring the backcountry, the best way to avoid avalanches is to choose a good route away from recognized dangers.

If avalanche terrain must be crossed, it is best to cross in the early morning, before sunup, or in the initial stages of a snowstorm. In a severe storm, hole up and give the snow a chance to settle.

To cross slide terrain, an easy downhill traverse across a clear area in the outrun (concave bottom portion) of the hill is best. To cross just below the crest (convex top portion) of a hill is dangerous.

When crossing a suspected slide path, loosen your ski bindings and take your hands out of the ski-pole straps. If you are wearing a parka with a hood, put it up and fasten it across your face to the eyes. Loosen cumbersome garments and items such as a backpack. Trail brightly colored avalanche cord behind you if possible.

Let one man cross on an easy traverse, gliding out of danger beyond the far side of the suspected avalanche's path. Others should follow, one at a time, in the first skier's tracks.

If caught in a moving snow mass, try not to panic. Ski to the side as quickly as possible. If that can't be done, get rid of your skis, poles and pack and try to stay on top of the snow by swimming, either in breaststroke fashion or on your back with your feet downhill. When the slide stops, clear an air space around your head and mouth immediately, for the snow will set hard at once.

If you see somebody caught, mark the last place you saw him, for the area of search will be below that spot. All should promptly assist in any search.

As more people travel into the backcountry, the possibility of somebody actually getting caught in a snowslide increases. During the 1972–73 ski season one woman was buried when she skied away from a regulation trail at Aspen, and another was swept under during a powder-snow expedition at Sun Valley. Both of these women were Alpine skiers and were extremely capable on the boards. Snowslides do occur, even at the better-known ski areas.

This doesn't mean you should never ski in the backcountry. But you should realize avalanches do catch people once in a while.

Using good judgment helps to prevent slide disasters. However, like the two skiers above, sometimes people are trapped, and they must be located immediately.

Most rescue groups employ surface searching, probing, or the use of trained dogs to find avalanche victims. Relatively new to the scene is an electronic locator called a Skadi, named after a Norse mythological figure who ran away from her husband, the giant Njörd, to be with the enchanter Ull.

The Skadi is a transmitter-receiver carried by each member of a touring party. Each skier turns the device on to transmit. If a person is caught by a snowslide, others switch their Skadis to receive, and search in a prescribed pattern. A Skadi-equipped party can search much faster than conventional probers. The signal can pass through some one hundred feet of snow, and one man receiving a signal can cover an area in the same time that six hundred probers can, according to a Swiss study. Drawbacks to the device are its cost (one hundred and ten dollars and up) and the fact that each person must carry one for best effect.

For more information you can write the manufacturer: Lawtronics Inc., 326 Walton Drive, Buffalo, New York, 14226.

There is also a similar device, called a Skilok, manufactured and sold by Sadler Associates, Ricksmanworth, England.

When skiing unfamiliar terrain, consult the Forest Service or the ski patrol near the area you want to tour. Any route selection should avoid as many hazards as possible.

Snow Safety: Preventive Measures

Whoever said "An ounce of prevention is worth a pound of cure" must have had ski-touring in mind. That sentence is the key to touring safely. A knowledge of what can happen in winter woods may save you many uncomfortable hours after a tour.

Remember, respect for nature will keep you aware of changing conditions while touring. Don't test the outdoors, because you can lose. After all, "It's not nice to fool Mother Nature!"

Take care of yourself, don't be careless or ignorant, and you will find the winter environment very friendly. Here are a few things you should be aware of to make your trips safer:

First Aid and First Aid Kit: Ski-touring isn't a dangerous sport. The number of serious accidents to Colorado touring skiers is almost nil. But although rare, accidents do happen, and you should be prepared.

Every touring group should have one person knowledgeable in first aid. There isn't a ski patrolman behind every tree in the backcountry. First-aid courses are given almost everywhere. Get in contact with your local Red Cross chapter or citizen safety group and take an advanced course. A first aid textbook can be obtained by writing the American Red Cross, Garden City, New York. Knowing what to do in the backcountry when a person is hurt may make the difference between a simple injury and a more serious one.

As a general rule, a first-aid kit should contain bandages, adhesive tape, adhesive pads, gauze patches, Band-Aids, sunburn cream, salt tablets, mirror, needle, razor blade and antiseptic.

Blisters: Blisters can occur while touring. To prevent them, make sure your boots and gloves fit properly. Boots should be well broken in for longer tours. When putting on touring shoes be certain your socks are not wrinkled. If you feel a boot or a glove is pinching or rubbing, stop skiing and protect the area with padded adhesive or moleskin. If you get a rubbing blister, prick it as soon as possible with a sterile needle, drain it, cover it with antiseptic, and pad the area with bandages.

Blistering may also result from severe sunburn or frostbite. Don't lance these skin injuries, because more damage may be done. See a doctor as soon as possible for treatment.

Frostbite: When out in cold weather, frostbite, which is a partial or total freezing of tissue, may occur to unprotected areas, for the most part feet, hands, ears and nose.

Cold injury begins with the cooling of the body. The brain then sends messages to increase blood flow — heat — to the cold areas. This would be recognized as rosy cheeks on a cold day.

If cold exposure continues, the brain sends messages to protect the vital organs, and blood flow is cut off to peripheral areas. The endangered tissue becomes cold, pale, and firm.

Frostbite generally occurs at any temperature thirty-two degrees Fahrenheit or lower. It can also take place at temperatures above freezing if the wind blows hard enough to bring the chill factor below the freezing point. Cold, wind, and moisture increase the chance of frostbite. The chart below shows the effects of cold and wind on a total exposure level, commonly referred to as the wind-chill factor.

If you read the wind-chill chart, you will see that at fourteen degrees Fahrenheit with a twenty-five-mile-an-hour wind the total exposure level is minus twenty-four degrees Fahrenheit.

To protect against frostbite, dress in layers, use mittens instead of gloves, and wear water-repellent — not waterproof — outer garments. The clothing layer next to the skin should absorb enough perspiration to keep you relatively dry and not clammy. Waterproof items tend to trap moisture, lowering body temperature. Cotton socks are good next to the feet, covered by a heavier wool pair. Tight boots and elastic around ankles and wrists are not good, because they can restrict circulation.

To keep body temperature up, keep moving. The natural touring stride should be enough to ward off frostbite. However, when in extremely cold weather and on a rest break, members of the group should watch each other's face for signs of "whiteness," indicating frostbite. These patches can be warmed gently at once and protected.

	LOCAL TEMPERATURE (°F)										
WIND SPEED (MPH)	32	23	14	5	− 4	−13	−22	− 31	− 40	− 49	− 58
	EQUIVALENT TEMPERATURE (°F)										
calm	32	23	14	5	− 4	−13	−22	− 31	− 40	− 49	− 58
5	29	20	10	1	− 9	−18	−28	− 37	− 47	− 56	− 65
10	18	7	− 4	−15	−26	−37	−48	− 59	− 70	− 81	− 92
15	13	− 1	−13	−25	−37	−49	−61	− 73	− 85	− 97	−109
20	7	− 6	−19	−32	−44	−57	−70	− 83	− 96	−109	−121
25	3	−10	−24	−37	−50	−64	−77	− 90	−104	−117	−130
30	1	−13	−27	−41	−54	−68	−82	− 97	−109	−123	−137
35	− 1	−15	−29	−43	−57	−71	−85	− 99	−113	−127	−142
40	− 3	−17	−31	−45	−59	−74	−87	−102	−116	−131	−145
45	− 3	−18	−32	−46	−61	−75	−89	−104	−118	−132	−147
50	− 4	−18	−33	−47	−62	−76	−91	−105	−120	−134	−148

LITTLE DANGER FOR PROPERLY CLOTHED PERSONS   CONSIDERABLE DANGER   VERY GREAT DANGER

DANGER FROM FREEZING OF EXPOSED FLESH

Wind-chill Chart

If you are severely frostbitten, there are several actions to follow:

— Don't thaw the part until you are sure no further damage can be done by repeated frostbite.
— Thaw the injured tissue at body temperature, between ninety-eight and one hundred degrees Fahrenheit. Don't warm the tissue excessively by placing the jeopardized area near intense heat of any kind, for it will burn the injured portion. A warm bath is good. Use a thermometer to check the temperature.
— Avoid intake of alcohol. It dilates arteries, increasing heat loss.
— Don't walk on or massage the frostbitten part.
— Don't rub the injured area with snow.

As the numb, frostbitten area returns to normal, there will probably be some pain and a pins-and-needles sensation.

Severe frostbite should be treated in a hospital. Doctors have had success in treating extreme cases by using new agents that assist the body in bringing blood — heat — to injured tissue. However, even with modern methods sometimes the victim is permanently damaged.

Hypothermia: Being in prolonged cold without proper clothing may result in a condition called "hypothermia," or "cold exposure." This happens when the body has been cooled to a point where its heat-regulation mechanism ceases to function. The person's body temperature then quickly drops to that of the environment, which can be fatal. Dress warmly to prevent cold exposure.

Hypothermia can take place without the victim first becoming frostbitten. If a person is frostbitten and begins to chill, it is crucial to warm him quickly. Get him out of the wind and into a shelter (behind a rock or a lean-to). If possible, build a fire and warm him in a sleeping bag next to another person. If you don't have a sleeping bag, cover the victim with extra clothing. Get him to take hot liquids.

Exhaustion: Exposure and exhaustion sometimes go hand in hand. Symptoms of exhaustion include complete fatigue, dizziness and unsteadiness. This condition is usually accompanied (and partially caused) by loss of body salt.

Excessive perspiration, with the accompanying loss of body salt, can be a prelude to exhaustion. To prevent this desalting condition, take salt tablets or drink a liquid that will also replace body salts. (Heavy intake of plain water has a tendency to dilute body salts.)

Snowblindness: Snowblindness is a burn of the cornea, usually by ultraviolet rays.

Dark glasses, which absorb ultraviolet light rays, should be worn to prevent snowblindness. On bright days, when light reflects off the snow, and especially in high altitudes, where dangerous rays are stronger, sunglasses are mandatory. You really have to be careless to become snowblind.

You probably won't know you are burning your eyes.

However, blurry vision and halos around light sources may be indicators.

The effects of snowblindness become noticeable some eight to ten hours after the eyes have been burned. They will feel as if sand has been rubbed into them. The victim should be treated by an eye doctor.

Sunburn: You can get burned in the mountains as easily as you can on the beach. Ultraviolet rays and the sun's rays reflecting from snow can cause burns in a matter of hours, even on cloudy days.

To prevent sunburn, apply a cream to exposed parts, especially nose and lips.

Common sense will keep most skiers out of trouble. Heed the body's natural warning systems. If you start feeling tired, slow down and take a break. Make the tour enjoyable, not impossible.

You will find that a moment of prevention is worth days of cure. Even though you must be aware of what can happen in a winter environment, remember that touring is a safe sport. The injuries described are rare and can be treated.

Path-Finding

There is little chance of getting lost on marked touring trails. However, the unexpected can happen, so here are a few suggestions if you become disoriented.

Being able to use map and compass is helpful, especially when skiing unfamiliar terrain. It is good to study maps before going into an area (see Chapter 7 for map and compass skills). And, if possible, keep a landmark in view during a tour to use as a point of reference.

If it isn't snowing, the first rule to follow when you think you may be lost is to turn around and return home by following the exact tracks you came in on. *Don't take short cuts!* If your path crosses other ski tracks, this little hint might be helpful: sometimes you can backtrack by noting the marks your ski poles made in the snow during your forward progress.

If you are caught in a large blizzard and your tracks are completely covered (this is very rare), you can use these general hints to find your way home:

— The sun rises in the east and sets in the west (basic knowledge but easy to forget if you become panicked).
— Bark is usually darker on the north side of a tree.
— At night (if the stars can be seen) the North Star can be found by locating the Big Dipper and looking down the "line" formed by the two end stars of its "bowl." The

North Star points generally in a northerly direction from most parts of the United States.

If you have no chance of finding a way out, prepare a camp immediately, while your energy level is still high and it is still light enough to see.

Sometimes when people are lost they try to guess a direction of travel. This is bad because you could get into more serious trouble than you are already in. In situations like this, it is better to stay where you are.

The Day Pack

To carry items for a tour, you should have some sort of a day pack. This can be a "fanny pack," which buckles around the waist, or a small backpack. There are numerous good, comfortable packs on the market.

Group items, such as food, should be divided among those going on the trip. A day pack might contain:

— Canteen or water bottle
— Food, including snacks
— First-aid kit
— Sunglasses
— Sun cream
— Matches
— Wax, scraper and cork
— Tools: screwdriver and pliers
— Knife
— A bit of wire
— Avalanche cord
— Flashlight
— Extra wool socks
— Extra ski tip (normally only one or two are needed to cover everybody in the tour)
— Camera and film

— Compass and map
— Room for clothing as you remove it

You will find these items can be fitted into a very small space, and you can add or subtract from the above list as your trip may require.

Length of Tour

The average day tour should be about five hours, including an hour for lunch. If you are on your skis by 9 A.M. you should plan to be back at 2 P.M., or 3 P.M. at the latest. This will still give you about two extra hours of daylight should you have some kind of trouble.

The average tour should include comfort stops as well as a lunch break. The camaraderie during these rests is an essential part of ski-touring. A trail stop gets the group (which may have become strung out along the route) together. During these times clothing can be adjusted, equipment fixed or changed, pictures taken, conversations held. Skiers may want to rewax during a break, observe an animal or bird, or just take in the scenery. It is a good time to have a snack of dried fruit or other quick-energy foods. Remember to wait for the last arrival to *rest* before taking off again.

Use a rotation system when breaking trail. The leader and stronger skiers may take their turn more often if they enjoy it or want to.

If a tour appears to be too long, be ready to abandon the goal and turn back to finish early. Often skiers bite off more than they can chew. Don't risk the health and safety of the group by trying to push too far.

Lunch Break

A gourmet lunch is easy to pack for a day tour. Sausages, beef and chicken, French bread, cheeses and wine are common and easy to carry. I have been on tours where skiers have produced portable stoves for hot lunches. With modern camping equipment almost anything is possible. You can get as basic or fancy as you wish.

One hint is to take more than you usually eat. Ski-touring burns up the calories, and an extra nibble may come in handy.

Choosing a lunch site is important. On a good day the picnic area should be in the sun and out of the wind. A scenic view is nice, and water and firewood nearby are helpful. On a snowy day head for the heavy timber or deep woods for protection from the elements.

Backcountry and woods are beautiful in the winter: seas of untracked snow, blue sky, and the wind whispering through the forest. Imagine the glistening white of the snow and the stark green and soft grays of trees, great bowls of snow funneling away to become lazy streams with dry gravel spits suitable for picnics. Sound beautiful? It is, and comfortable, too.

Dry logs can be used for chairs and tree stumps for back rests. You can also make a dry, comfortable seat or back rest with your skis. Place the ski tips in the wrist loops of upright poles, the ski tails in the snow. Sit on your rucksack, extra clothing, "space blanket" (they are lightweight and

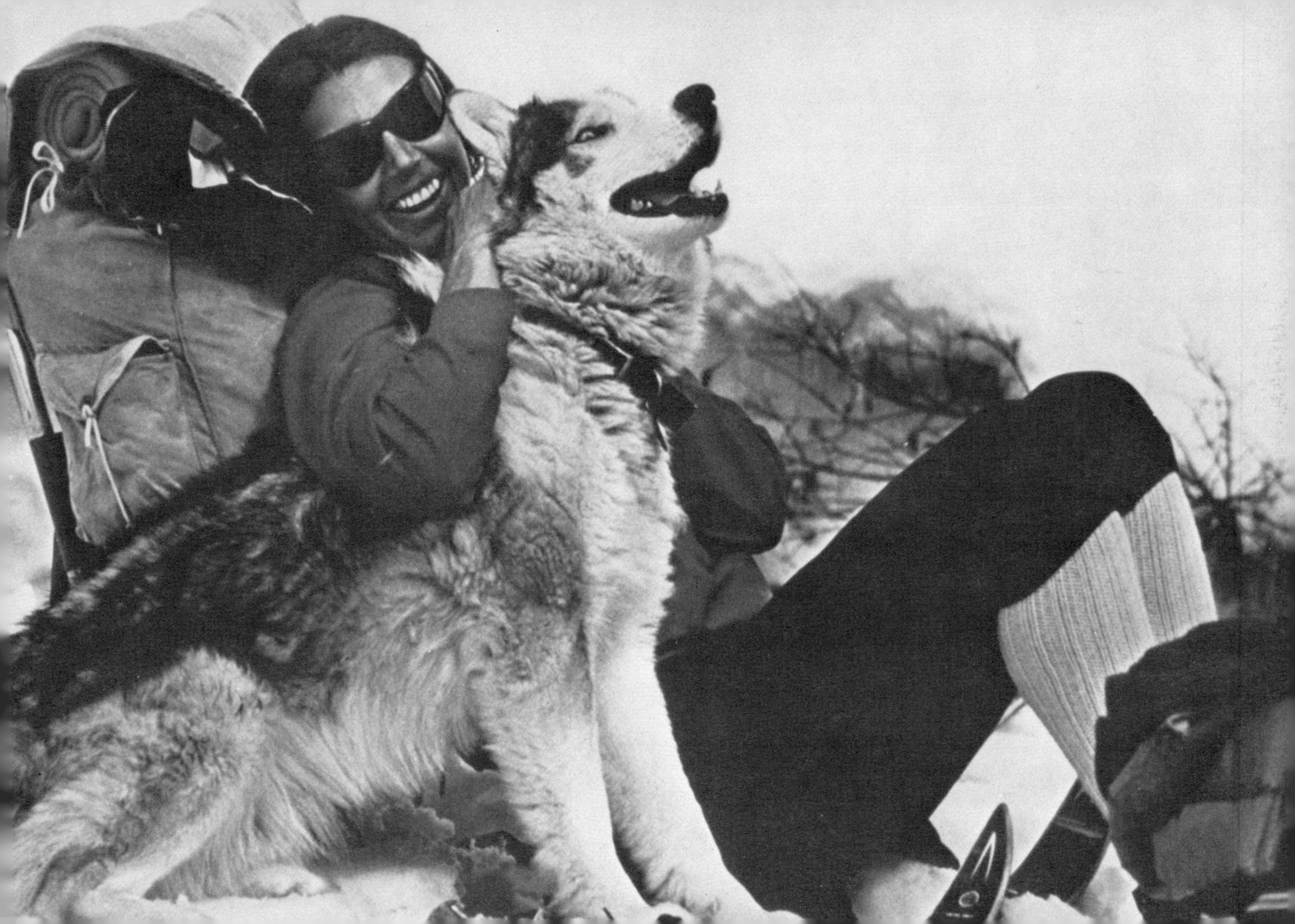

easy to carry), or a log and put your back against your skis, face to the sun — that's living!

Trail Skills

Anybody who has been touring for a few years has probably picked up a few trail skills to make his journey easier. I will list a few hints I consider important. Some of these can be used every trip.

Bumps and Dips: A skier who knows how to utilize terrain is well on his way to enjoyable touring. If technique is used properly in these areas, more speed can be obtained with little effort.

Any slight or sizable roll in the terrain is a bump that can be used to your advantage. The trick is to push off the bump with one ski just as it begins to slope downward, like a sprinter leaving the starting block. Timing is the key to this technique.

Where there are bumps there are usually dips. To increase speed, push down in the low part of the dip with a ski and then spring out. The resulting forward thrust is similar to squeezing a watermelon seed until it pops forward.

You can build bicycle bumps, which are a series of exaggerated, alternating humps along a regular touring track, and such a run may be used to practice bump-and-dip-terrain technique. As one ski goes over a bump, the other is going through a dip. For the next kick the process is reversed. To an onlooker the skiing motion resembles a pedaling bicyclist.

Stability: When stability is needed, you can widen the normal gap between your skis to four or six inches. Still feeling shaky? Add a telemark.

Dry Skis: Keeping the bottoms of your skis dry is important. If you should slip on a snow bridge and get your skis wet from a stream, *immediately* ski into fresh, dry snow at a fast pace, forcing the skis to slide. The snow will absorb the moisture instead of it freezing on the bottoms of your skis.

In the spring, it is important to have a well-pine-tarred base if you have wooden skis. This will prevent the wood from soaking up water and make it easier to apply wax. A wet ski will have very little glide, like trying to slide on a sponge.

Cleaning the Bottoms: If you should happen to collect ice or snow on the bottom of your skis, you will have to scrape it off before the ski will slide properly. One way to do this is to slide your skis back and forth across a dead branch until the running surface is clean. If you have a friend with you, ask him to step across the track and edge his skis. Slide your skis over his. To avoid scratching the friend's skis, use caution, especially if your skis have metal edges. You can always kick a ski up on its tail and have a friend clean the surface with a scraper.

Avoiding Broken Ski Tips: Sharp drop-offs and dips, ditches, stream beds and wind-packed snowdrifts are good places to break a ski tip. Approach these areas on the bias to reduce the angle of attack. This will place much less strain on the ski.

If you break a tip, you can use an extra glove to cover the splintered portion. At least it will get you home if you have forgotten to bring an emergency ski tip with you.

Protecting Eyes: When touring in a thickly wooded area it is advisable to wear some kind of eye protection, such as sunglasses or goggles, to keep twigs or low-hanging branches from injuring an eye.

Preventing Arm Injury: When skiing downhill through trees and/or in deep snow, remove pole straps from wrists. If the pole gets tangled in a tree or caught in the snow, let go of it. You can retrieve it later.

Breaking Trail: You may find that breaking trail two or three days after a snowstorm is easier where the snow has melted during the day and refrozen at night, a process that gradually settles the snow, forming a base. Such conditions are more likely to be found on slopes with a southern exposure than slopes with a northern exposure, and are also more common in dry-snow areas.

The Wool-Sock Trick: On extended trips in cold weather, you can add much more warmth to your feet and keep your boots a lot drier by stretching heavy wool socks *over* your ski boots.

The Half Ski Pole: When climbing a fairly steep traverse, especially when carrying a pack, use only one-half of a ski pole on the uphill for better balance. To do this, grip the uphill pole in the center.

The Water Basket: An easy way to get a drink of water from a stream (make sure the water is pure) is to collect a pile of snow on a ski-pole basket and lower the pole into some quiet water. The snow will absorb the water. Then lift the pole from the stream or lake and suck the water from the snow. No muss, no fuss.

For years I understood this to be an old Indian trick until one of my students asked me if Indians had done much ski-touring.

The Night Tour and Other Tours

Skiing at night can be a thrill. If there is a full moon and you know the trail well, head lamps won't be necessary. But for most night tours, the battery-operated miner's headlight is good to have.

Scout the terrain before the tour. Make sure it is easy skiing and a short trip. Have a good supply of firewood handy if you plan to have a night picnic and fire.

Nighttime changes the mood of any adventure. A roaring fire, a warm drink, hot sausages, music (find somebody who plays a concertina or accordion), and you will enjoy an unforgettable experience.

Remember, when skiing downhill in the night, it is hard to see terrain changes and dangerous obstacles like rocks and stumps. Be careful, and keep the speed down, because the snow will more than likely be much faster.

There are several other kinds of tours that can be taken. In some national parks, such as Grand Teton, Wyoming; Yellowstone, Montana; and Yosemite, California, there are regular, free, ranger-led tours. These parks, along with Rocky Mountain National Park in Colorado, have lots of wild animals to photograph. Of these, Yellowstone is probably the most spectacular for photographic game tours.

There are high-country tours for those in the mountains and river tours for those near waterways. And there is the sought-after deep-powder trip.

Some enthusiasts scout country on foot during the summer, discovering trails and stockpiling food for touring in the winter.

Because skis are a quiet mode of travel, it is possible to get very close to game animals, birds and other wildlife. Don't scare or chase the animals; they have a hard enough time surviving in winter without having to run through belly-deep snow to avoid human intruders. Boning up on what animals look like with their winter fur on, and the tracks they make, can increase the enjoyment of a tour.

Some woods and forests are full of ghost towns. These are exciting to see in winter and imagine how they must have been as thriving communities.

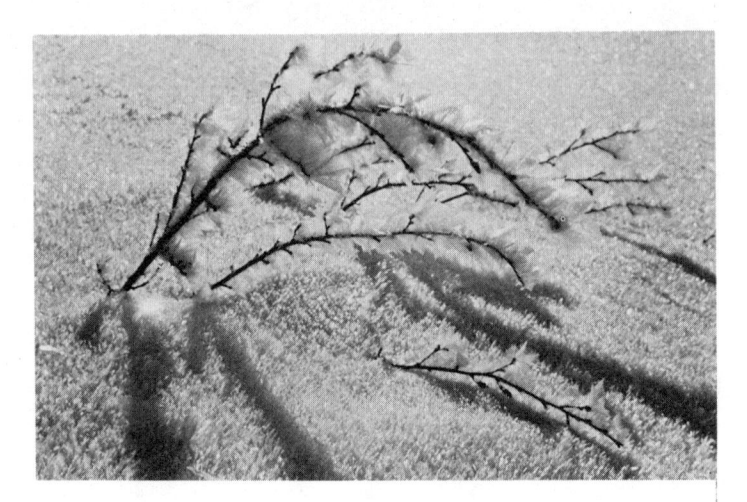

5 | More on Equipment, Clothing and Waxing

Introduction

For the novice skier, the array of ski equipment available in sports shops might cause some bewilderment. There are many kinds of skis, poles, boots, bindings and clothing. From this huge selection, a beginner is asked to purchase gear that will give him the best performance for the money he wants to spend.

How do you sift through the many choices and come up with an outfit that will fit your needs? I believe the beginner should know some of the basic rules to help in his selection, and then he should consult a professional. The pros know the best equipment to match with your experience for the terrain you will be skiing. For example, a person touring on heavy midwestern or eastern snow might use a narrower ski than a person skiing western powder. The mountain skier might use a wider ski in the soft snow.

I can give you basic information about the length and materials of skis, the types of bindings for particular boots, and the different kinds of ski poles.

Skis

Generally, the touring ski should be flexible, and if wooden, have as an option metal or compressed hardwood (lignostone) edges. Some manufacturers are producing good metal and fiberglass skis with metal edges the full length of the ski.

With wooden skis there are three basic things to consider: the number of laminations (the more the better), the type of wood, and the craftsmanship.

When there is a greater number of laminations, the ski designer can control the flex pattern, thus insuring that the ski will bend the right amount in the correct places. This will give you a ski that will perform better under all conditions. More laminations also means increased strength and durability.

Generally, stronger woods are used for the outside and running surface of a ski. Softer woods and special glues are used for interior laminations. In most wooden skis, a birch or hickory is used for the base. Birch will hold a wax better and is lighter, but tends to wear out faster than the tougher, heavier hickory. Even some metal and fiberglass skis use wood interiors and bottoms. Proper wood plus good craftsmanship add up to a high-quality ski.

If you are serious about the sport and can afford to spend the extra ten to fifteen dollars for the better boards, I believe it is well worth the extra money. Chances for breakage are less and the quality is superior. A pair of wooden skis can cost anywhere from forty to ninety dollars.

Fiberglass and synthetic skis have recently proven to be superior in many ways: they are lighter and stronger. The camber can be set and controlled more easily, they can be produced more uniformly to make a matched pair. The skis very seldom break. They won't soak up water and they are faster in wet snow. The new plastic bottoms have eliminated the process of pine tarring or applying Grundvalla base wax, and many do not require wax at all.

The production and sales of fiberglass and synthetic skis has risen sharply during the last two years, and their unit cost has decreased. In some cases it doesn't cost any more to buy a good synthetic ski at seventy-five to one hundred twenty dollars than it does top of the line wood skis.

The non-wax synthetic ski is in more demand in some parts of the country than the top wood ski. On a non-wax ski the potential running surfaces are the step-method, the fish-scale and the imitation Mohair strip. If you are strictly opposed to learning about wax or applying it, then these non-wax skis are the ski for you. The efficiency of these non-wax skis is improving but the wax-type synthetic ski still offers you better performance because you are able to wax for specific snow conditions. Check with your local touring-pro shop to find out the best type of non-wax ski for your part of the country.

Kinds of Skis, Including Length and Camber

A ski consists of a tip, the upturned front part, and at the opposite end, a tail. The area just behind the tip is called the shovel, while the section in the middle is called the waist. Skis are usually measured for width at the waist.

There are essentially four types of cross-country/touring skis, differentiated by width.

In some instances a ski's width and the classification mentioned below won't match. The discrepancy is due to the special manufacturing considerations of individual companies, for each has its own pattern and design for ski construction. Therefore, the following classifications for the width of cross-country and touring skis are approximations.

The thinnest and lightest ski is the cross-country. Approximately 47 to 52 millimeters wide, it is feather light, can break easily, and is made to be skied in a prepared track when racing or training.

The light touring ski is a little wider (about 50 to 55 millimeters), quite a bit stronger, and a popular ski for people who tour in valley floors, rolling hills and/or the well-packed snow conditions generally found in the Midwest and East.

In the mountainous areas the most popular choice is the general touring ski (width, about 55 to 60 millimeters). I recommend this one for people who want to learn to ski downhill on touring gear, in addition to doing regular touring. It also handles well in powder.

Left to right: cross-country racing ski, light touring ski, general touring ski, mountain touring ski.

Another type is the mountain touring ski (approximately 60 to 68 millimeters wide). It is the heaviest of the touring skis, and many times will have a full-length steel edge. Ski-mountaineering, as I mentioned earlier, usually consists of skiers carrying heavy rucksacks over alpine glaciers and snow fields. This is really a specialty ski.

For most touring skiers I recommend the light or general touring ski.

Ski Length: If you are a beginner and are going to buy skis, the rule of thumb mentioned in Chapter 1 applies. Advanced or expert skiers can choose a length they like.

Camber: There are two kinds of camber, or bow, in a ski. When a ski is placed flat on a floor, the distance from the center of its bottom to the floor is known as "bottom camber." Manufacturers build bottom camber into a ski to distribute the skier's weight evenly over the entire ski and to achieve desired tracking characteristics. When purchasing a pair of skis, check to be sure that bottom camber is relatively the same for each ski.

Place a pair of skis side by side flat on a floor with the shovels touching and the tails together. The space between the skis at the waist is known as the "cut" or "side camber." Side camber facilitates the turning ability of the ski.

NOTE: When buying a pair of skis, always check to make sure you have a factory pair by matching the serial numbers.

Boots

For general touring, the boot should resemble a flexible-soled, water-resistant, lightweight hiking boot. It should have a square toe to give lateral support when secured in a touring binding.

There are several kinds of bindings, and generally, the stiffer-soled or heavier the boot, the heavier the binding you will want. Therefore, you should select a boot first and then a binding. Let's look at some touring boots and then link them to bindings.

Ski-touring boots are classed as the cross-country racing shoe (lightest), light touring boot, general touring boot and mountaineering boot. Cross-country footwear, which is light, low-cut, and very flexible, is designed for training or racing in a prepared track. This shoe generally costs about twenty-five to forty dollars. This style, it might be added, isn't especially warm for touring.

The light touring boot has more support, a stiffer sole, and allows for increased ankle and foot control. The average cost should be twenty-five to thirty-five dollars.

The general touring boot is more shoe than the light touring boot. General touring footwear is heavier and usually has a stiffer counter in the heel section and a thicker sole, which gives more lateral control. Often, this boot is lined with leather or has some kind of fur for added comfort and warmth. Also, it has a higher cut to cover the ankle. If you are planning to learn downhill skiing on your touring

Left to right: cross-country racing boot, light touring boot, general touring boot, mountain boot. Boot in foreground shows the three holes for the pin-type binding.

equipment, I recommend this boot because of the additional support, which in turn will give you greater ski control. Cost of the general touring boot varies from twenty-five to forty-five dollars, depending on the quality. The mountain boot is usually a hiking or rock-climbing shoe with a round toe. This boot is worn primarily by backpackers and mountaineers touring the high mountain country. Its cost ranges between twenty and eighty dollars. The fit of a cross-country racing shoe should be snug with one pair of socks. Circulation from hard running or training will keep your feet warm. The fit of a light or general touring boot should be comfortable with two pairs of socks. Tight boots will cut off blood flow to your feet, causing them to get cold.

Bindings

Boots more than anything else determine the kind of binding a person should have. For the skier who has chosen the cross-country racing shoe or light touring boot, a toe binding such as a Rotefella (about seven dollars) is recommended. These bindings are sometimes called "rattrap" or pin-type bindings.

Ski companies are now producing step-in and pinless toe bindings (about nine dollars). The step-in could restrict you to the use of one brand of boot because the toe plate that fits one company's binding might not fit another manufacturer's toepiece. But a step-in works well for a person satisfied with one combination of boot and binding.

To date, toe bindings come in two or three sizes to fit different-width boots, so make certain you get the correct width for your boot. Industry recognizes this unnecessary complication in the sport and is now working hard to standardize boots so all will fit one binding size.

Most of these bindings function equally well, but some are easier to put on and take off. Outside of the step-ins, I recommend a binding with a fastener that has good leverage to make it easier to manage.

For a heavy person, or someone with a large foot using the general touring boot, I suggest a light, cable-type binding for more strength, such as a Kandahar (about ten dollars) or a heavy toe binding. I have known strong skiers to rip apart a light "rattrap" wearing a stiffer-soled shoe.

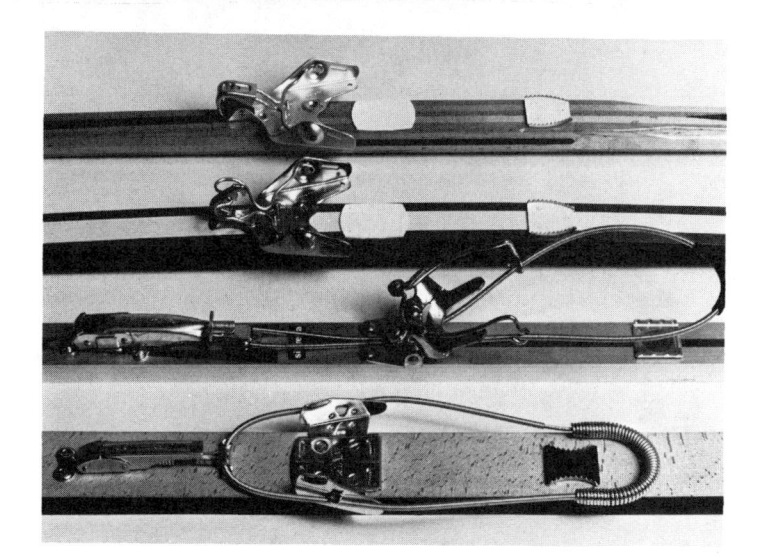

Top to bottom: step-in toe binding, pin-type (Rotefella) binding, Silvretta binding for mountain boots, light cable binding.

The cable binding may come with side hitches to secure the boot to the ski. I am strongly against this type of tie-down for safety reasons. A fixed heel definitely increases the chances of injury.

A special binding, called the Silvretta (about twenty dollars), is specially made for the round-toed mountaineering boot. This is a very strong, heavy-duty binding designed for ski-mountaineering.

Ski-touring bindings run from seven to ten dollars. Ski-mountaineering bindings are often more than twenty dollars.

Heel Plates

There are several items that are placed on top of the ski behind the binding to support the heel of the boot and keep snow from clinging to it. These are called heel plates.

Some are tiny pyramids that fit into a notch at the back of the heel; others are metal squares with serrated edges and rubber centers. Both of these are good, but I especially recommend any that have the serrated edges.

Heel attachments that lock the heel of the boot to the ski should be avoided.

Ski Poles

Touring poles are made of bamboo (tonkin cane), fiberglass, or metal. They should be flexible and light, and should measure three to four inches below the shoulder when placed in an upright position on the ground. After you have had some touring experience, you may want to choose a pole that varies a few inches from this general standard.

For skiing in soft snow, the ski-pole basket should be about five inches in diameter. This is sometimes known as a powder ring. Poles used for racing have smaller baskets.

Some poles, especially from the Scandinavian countries, have as an option an adjustable wrist strap on the handle. I believe this added advantage is worth the increased cost of about a dollar-fifty. The adjustable strap will allow you to wear heavy mittens during the colder months, and when tightened, lighter gloves in warmer weather.

The most commonly used touring pole is the bamboo. This material is relatively inexpensive, has good resilience, and although very lightweight, still is limber enough to give you an active pole. If it splits, it can be repaired with plastic or a good adhesive tape. Bamboo poles cost approximately six-fifty to eight-fifty a pair.

Fiberglass touring poles are a little heavier than bamboo and usually are more expensive.

Metal and metal-alloy poles, which are being produced by some of the leading manufacturers, are light, strong and have a good kick action (the quick spring back from a bending position). They are a quality pole and are now being used by some of America's top cross-country racers. Cost can average from twelve to twenty-eight dollars a pair, but they will perform well with little or no breakage.

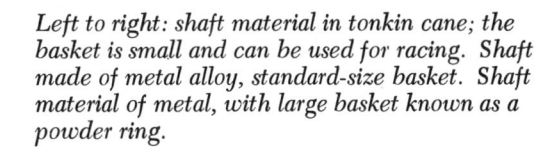

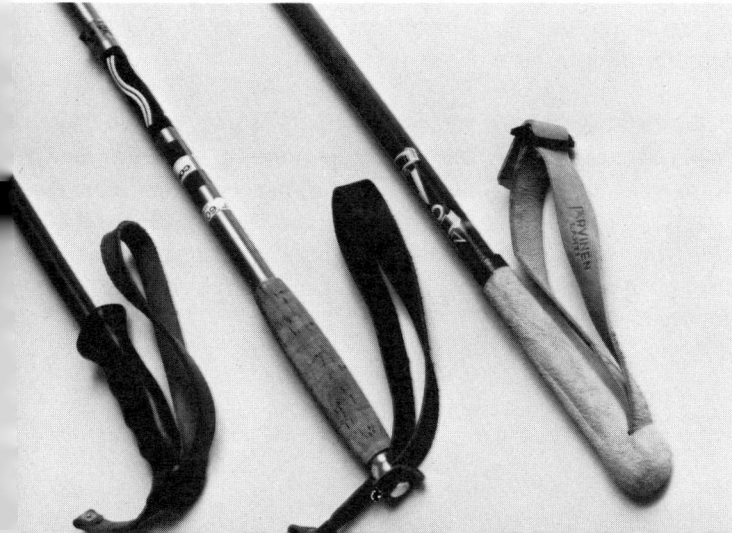

Left to right: shaft material in tonkin cane; the basket is small and can be used for racing. Shaft made of metal alloy, standard-size basket. Shaft material of metal, with large basket known as a powder ring.

Left to right: rubber handle, cork handle, leather handle. All these poles have adjustable wrist straps.

Clothing

Clothing should be chosen for freedom of movement, comfort and warmth. Materials such as dungaree — which soaks up moisture — and tight stretch fabrics — which hamper movement — should be avoided. Wool, or combinations of wool and another material, can be very good. I lean towards wool because it can keep you warm even if it gets wet.

Dressing from the Waist Down

Long Underwear: I prefer cotton for its absorbent qualities, or a fishnet fabric with air pockets for insulation and evaporation. Both work well to keep you from getting clammy damp while touring. Priced from five to fifteen dollars.

Knee Socks: I recommend wool. These should come well over the knee, not just below, so a knicker knee strap can help hold up the sock. Priced from five to fifteen dollars. A pair of wool or cotton socks (about two dollars) can be worn beneath the knee socks to help keep feet warm.

Pants: Knickers are preferable, either wool, rayon, corduroy or poplin. They cost from fifteen to fifty dollars. A loose-fitting trouser will also do.

Gaiters: Gaiters, or snow spats, made of a water-repellent material, are usually worn in deep snow to keep the fluff from working inside the boot top. They come in various lengths, depending on snow depth and how much protection you want. They should provide a snug fit around the lower leg and cover the boot at the ankle. Priced from five to fifteen dollars.

Dressing from the Waist Up

A T-Shirt: Cotton recommended, two dollars.

A Long-Sleeved Fishnet Shirt or Turtleneck T-Shirt: five to ten dollars.

A Wool Shirt: Five to twenty dollars.

Wind Shirt or Parka Shell: Ten to twenty dollars.

Tightly Knit Sweater: Fifteen to fifty dollars.

Parka: Down-filled with hood recommended, but any warm, durable one is fine. Priced from twenty to sixty dollars.

Alternating Layers

The wool shirt, wind shirt or parka shell, sweater and parka provide layers of clothing that can be alternated to provide warmth and dryness for all types of activity and in all kinds of weather. Dressing in layers is the important key to staying comfortable.

Gear for Hands and Head

Mittens or gloves, either wool or leather, whichever you prefer, may be worn. Mittens are usually warmer. The hat should provide covering for the ears, and there are some that fold out into a face mask. This kind of hat is sometimes called a "Balaclava." Dark goggles or sunglasses are necessary on bright days. Avoid tight straps around wrists and ankles, for they can hamper circulation to hands and feet, causing them to chill.

Touring is a warm sport. Body movement will give you good blood flow and keep you warm. In most conditions, skiers begin a trip wearing a parka and shortly thereafter remove the coat and ski in a sweater. During nice weather it is common to see people standing around in sweaters and shirts, without hat or gloves!

Equipment Care

Remember, when ski-touring, your equipment is your best friend. Take good care of it. During the season be sure to wipe your skis off after each trip and store them in a dry place. Make sure the skis aren't cracked, especially around the tip. Check your bindings for damage and tighten all loose screws.

If you have leather boots, it is good to polish or wax them once in awhile and to melt some "snow seal" into the stitching around the boot soles. If your boots become wet, dry them slowly so they won't crack. Stuff them with newspaper and let them stand in a warm room overnight.

Check your ski poles for weakness and repair any damage. You can wind some adhesive tape between the joints of a bamboo pole for added strength. Try putting on some extra tape as you wind, so if you do happen to crack or break a pole in the backcountry, you will have some tape to repair it.

If you carry a little pack of any kind, add to it an extra pole basket and a small piece of wire. Extra baskets, like extra ski tips, can really come in handy if you have a breakdown.

When the snow melts, store your equipment in a cool, dry place. Next winter, if your skis are wooden, you might want to put fresh pine tar on the bottoms. This will put some life back in the wood and give you a good wax binder to start the season.

All-Important Wax

Wax, along with equipment and clothing, is essential to ski-touring, especially if you want to become proficient in the sport.

You have had an introduction to elementary waxing and have probably realized it can be a fun part of the sport. Most general touring skiers enjoy the challenge of figuring out the most appropriate wax for the snow conditions and temperature of the day. Lively discussion will sometimes revolve around what wax to use, but usually the choice is easy.

About Wax

Experts argue about what causes the skis to hold when weighted and slide when moved. The majority opinion seems to be this: if it is waxed properly, minute snow crystals penetrate the wax on a motionless, weighted ski, giving the proper hold for the particular situation — either climbing or skiing over the flat. When that bond is broken the ski will slide.

If the skis are poorly waxed, they either won't hold because they are too slippery or will stick constantly and not glide at all. I have had skiers come to me with snow caked all over the bottoms of their skis, and I presume they had a wax with enough hold to climb the side of a building.

Without getting into the chemistry of wax, let's say it has amazing qualities, and in my estimation, it is worth your time to learn something about the basics of waxing.

Base Wax

Before a *running wax* is applied to skis with wooden bottoms, the running surface should have a *base wax* of pine tar, or a manufactured base coating commonly called Grundvalla. The base wax waterproofs wooden bottoms, provides a binder for the touring wax, and helps prevent the wood from drying out.

Tars can be applied in three different ways: spray-on, wipe-on, and warm-in. The spray-on and wipe-on methods, which are cold applications, will not last as long as the warm-in method.

To prepare your skis for base wax be sure they are clean of old wax or the factory finish. This is usually done by scraping the ski or by using a solvent or a wax remover. Then follow the directions for the kind of tar you have.

With warm-in varieties the substance is usually brushed on and heated into the ski with a blowtorch or small waxing torch until the tar begins to bubble, signifying the wood is absorbing the compound. Keep the torch moving *at all times* so as not to burn or scorch the wood. Remove excess tar with a rag before it has a chance to cool completely.

When the base is properly finished you can rub a hand over it without picking up any pine tar. The base should feel dry.

If your skis have the kind of plastic base that will hold running wax, you can eliminate base waxing. Industry is working hard to produce more advanced materials that will eliminate base-wax preparation. As these surfaces reach the marketplace, pine tar and Grundvalla will be used less and less.

Running Waxes

There are two basic categories of running waxes: hard and soft.

The hard waxes, with texture similar to a candle, are used for soft snow conditions.

The soft waxes, also known as klisters, have a texture similar to honey and are used for hard or harsh snow conditions, such as wet, granular, crusty and/or ice.

The hard waxes themselves are divided into two categories: the cold-color waxes and the warm-color waxes. Cold colors, in low to high temperature order, are black, light green, green, and blue. These waxes are used for new or old soft-snow conditions.

Warm-color waxes, in low to high temperature order, are purple, or red-blue, red and yellow. These waxes are used for new-fallen, wet snow that has a high water content.

Klisters are also color-coded: blue for ice, purple for soft mush, red for wet slush. (Some manufacturers have a yellow and a silver klister that correspond to the red-wet snow conditions.)

Directions on each wax container will tell you the snow conditions and snow temperatures under which the wax should be used. Experience will provide you with further knowledge and the skill to wax properly in all conditions.

Here is a helpful hint: Pick one manufacturer's wax and learn its characteristics. Don't buy a different brand for every outing, for each company's wax acts a little differently.

Beginners will find that just a few waxes are needed to cover most skiing conditions. Racers and experts find that more combinations and different kinds suit them better because minutes and seconds over a course are very important, or they are trying to attain perfection through extensive experiments. For their kind of waxing a vast amount of knowledge and experience is required. A few of the items taken into consideration by a cross-country racer are: condition of the track, water content of the snow, type of snow crystals, the skier's technique, different waxes for different parts of a course, how a wax will wear, and how it is applied (rough, smooth, painted, rubbed or ironed).

The average touring skier, however, need only be interested in a wax that works reasonably well in most conditions. So I have tried to simplify the selection procedure. Pick out two or three waxes that are commonly used in your area and experiment with them. You will get different results from using just one wax, depending on how you apply it: rough, rubbed out, or ironed smooth! Generally speaking, the smoother the wax, the more glide with less hold. With rough application the opposite is true.

I will tell you why just a few waxes should work. In the Rocky Mountains, an average winter temperature range might be from thirty to five degrees Fahrenheit, with the snow basically dry. Ninety percent of all skiing conditions in the Rockies fall into this category, which calls for only two waxes — hard blue for temperatures close to thirty degrees Fahrenheit and hard green for temperatures close to five degrees Fahrenheit.

These two waxes are interchangeable: you don't have to remove one to apply the other.

In the Midwest, skiers use different waxes because the snow usually has a higher water content. In the East, skiers lean toward soft waxes, or klisters, because of the lower elevation, as compared to the Rockies, and the greater moisture content of the snow, which causes coarser, or more granular, snow.

If you are in doubt about the waxes to use in your particular area, consult a touring professional or a touring specialty shop for information on local snow conditions.

The reason the touring skier can use fewer waxes than the racers is explained by the term "latitude," the temperature range in which a wax may be used. For example, the racing skier might use a hard blue only between twenty-five and twenty-eight degrees Fahrenheit, in soft snow with relatively little water content. The wax would be ironed on and smoothed by hand to suit the racer.

In contrast, the touring skier with the same snow conditions might use hard blue from five to thirty-two degrees Fahrenheit, and the way the wax is applied to the ski isn't nearly as critical. For general touring I recommend applying a colder wax first, and then, if it slips, putting on a small amount of the next-warmer colored wax under the center part of the ski, known as the "kicker area." Most major wax companies use the color code we talk about.

Waxing the Groove

Paraffin or silicone should be used in the groove of the ski. Never use a running wax of any kind in the groove, because it will have a tendency to ice up.

Klisters

Soft waxes, or klisters, are most often used in the spring, when the snow is soft and slushy under a bright sun. However, there is a special ice klister ("skare klister") used for frozen snow, which has a high water content. Such a condition might exist when a freeze sets in after a rain or a good thaw.

When applying klister, the cardinal rule is to put it on sparingly. Because the wax usually comes out of the tube easily, it is possible to get too much on your skis.

To maintain flow, the wax must be warm. If you are careful, you can squeeze one continuous stream of wax on each side of the groove on the bottom of the ski and smooth it out with an applicator (a Popsicle stick will do). Klister can also be painted on after heating it to a thin liquid. But for touring, the first method is sufficient.

Klister is a gooey, runny wax and can spill onto the sides of a ski. To make cleaning spills easy, run a little paraffin over the side walls of your ski *before* you wax with the klister. Then runovers can easily be peeled off. But if you use a little care, klister waxing can be done without mishap. After application, let the skis cool a couple of minutes before putting them on the snow.

Interchangeable Waxes

There is one more thing the general touring skier should know about waxes. Some waxes are interchangeable and can be applied over another; others are not.

The cold-color hard waxes are interchangeable, as are the warm-color ones. But a cold-color wax and a warm-color wax are not interchangeable.

All klisters could be interchangeable, but it usually isn't necessary to switch from one to another for touring.

This information should give you a hint about when you might want to use interchangeable waxes — in varying snow conditions on days when shady areas are colder than sunny areas. A little familiarity with waxes will result in successful application.

Waxless Skis

Science and industry are working to produce a waxless ski that will meet acceptable standards for the touring enthusiast. How far away is success? I don't know, but can speculate it will be soon. There are experimental models already on snow, some of which I am testing, that work reasonably well.

Two of the experimental skis might be of interest. One has a fish-scale bottom, which is a series of small half-moon cuts or serrations in a special plastic base. The effect resembles fish scales. The ski slides forward fairly well and holds reasonably well for the kick in most snow conditions.

Another waxless ski consists of thin, imitation mohair strips that are recessed in the base and placed in the center third of the ski. The fibers hold when the kick is applied, but they lie flat when sliding. This is a modern adaptation of a climber.

Independent studies done in Switzerland reveal that the relatively rougher no-wax surface reduces the glide to about sixty percent of that of a properly waxed ski.

However, as refinements are made, it seems likely waxless skis will be used more and more for touring. This could happen within the next year. Until then, the skier with an interest in new developments need be concerned only with applying running waxes to the recently developed plastic-base skis mentioned earlier.

The plastic touring base and the similar P-Tex base used on downhill skis have one thing in common: they are generally fast in most snow conditions. Therefore, with the new plastic base, a touring skier should have to wax only the center third of the ski for hold in most conditions.

Top to bottom: mountain touring ski with a sealskin climber attached; fish-scale bottom; P-Tex bottom with imitation mohair strips on each side of the groove, placed in the center third of the ski; Cross-Tex plastic base (made to hold touring wax) with thin aluminum edges for downhill skiing; wooden bottom with a pine-tar base.

When Not To Wax

You might want to begin a tour with an unwaxed ski. I know some pros who almost always give their skis a chance first before applying wax, especially if they start just before sunup.

When the sun appears, either at sunrise or from behind a cloud, the snow surface may change, and your hold and glide may become less effective. The first inclination is to stop and apply wax, or if you have already waxed, to change. But my advice is to keep moving. Make your skis work with the best technique possible. It takes about ten minutes for the surface of the snow to change, and during this period, practically no kind of wax will be effective because only a thin surface layer is warmed, while the snow beneath remains cold.

When the snow has made a definite, in-depth, temperature change, then you can decide whether or not to wax for the new snow. Learning when not to wax is as important as learning how to wax.

Giving the Wax a Chance

One thing that can happen if you are new to waxing is failure to give the wax you have chosen enough time to start working. Wax can take up to two hundred yards of moving contact with the snow (or about five minutes) before it starts reacting properly. Changing wax every couple of hundred feet reduces the enjoyment of any trip.

Removing Wax

If you have waxed your skis with hard blue one day, and the same conditions exist next time out, you will not have to wax. If, however, conditions have changed, you might want to put on a different wax. This means in most instances removing the old hard blue.

Hard waxes are easily removed with a scraper. To remove a klister, heat it with a torch and wipe it off with a clean rag. Remember to keep the torch moving at all times. Solvents can be used to remove both hard and klister waxes, but use caution with flammable liquids.

Cleaning agents such as acetone, if improperly used, can remove not only wax but also pine tar and plastic. Follow cleaning and skiing manufacturers' directions to the letter when removing wax.

The Wax Kit

There are several wax kits on the market, and the beginning skier might want to get one containing the waxes most often used in his area. Avoid a kit with about five different kinds of klisters and no hard waxes.

The kit should contain two or three hard waxes, a klister or two, a cork and scraper. You might want to add a small piece of paraffin. It's a good idea to carry klister in a sealed container to prevent leakage in your pack.

Front to rear: cork for use with hard wax, combination cork and scraper, black applicator for the klister wax, four containers of hard wax, a can of pine tar, a can of Grundvalla, a Swix wax kit, a tube of soft wax (klister), a spare tip, saw and small shovel, a normal-size day pack.

Technique and Waxing

Good technique and good waxing go together. When both are working well, you can amaze yourself by the ease with which you can go uphill and yet slide over the flat. But what happens when you get to the top of a nice powder slope and can do only snowplow turns to ski down? Ever see those snow snakes who leave figure eights in the fluff? Ever want to join them? You can, with a little practice on advanced downhill technique.

To set the scene . . . The day is bright and fresh, light snow covers the countryside. Hard blue wax holds well for the kick and when climbing. Your group chooses a tour that will include a couple of miles of downhill powder.

Now is the time you want to be able to ski parallel.

135

6 Advanced Downhill Technique, Including Powder Skiing

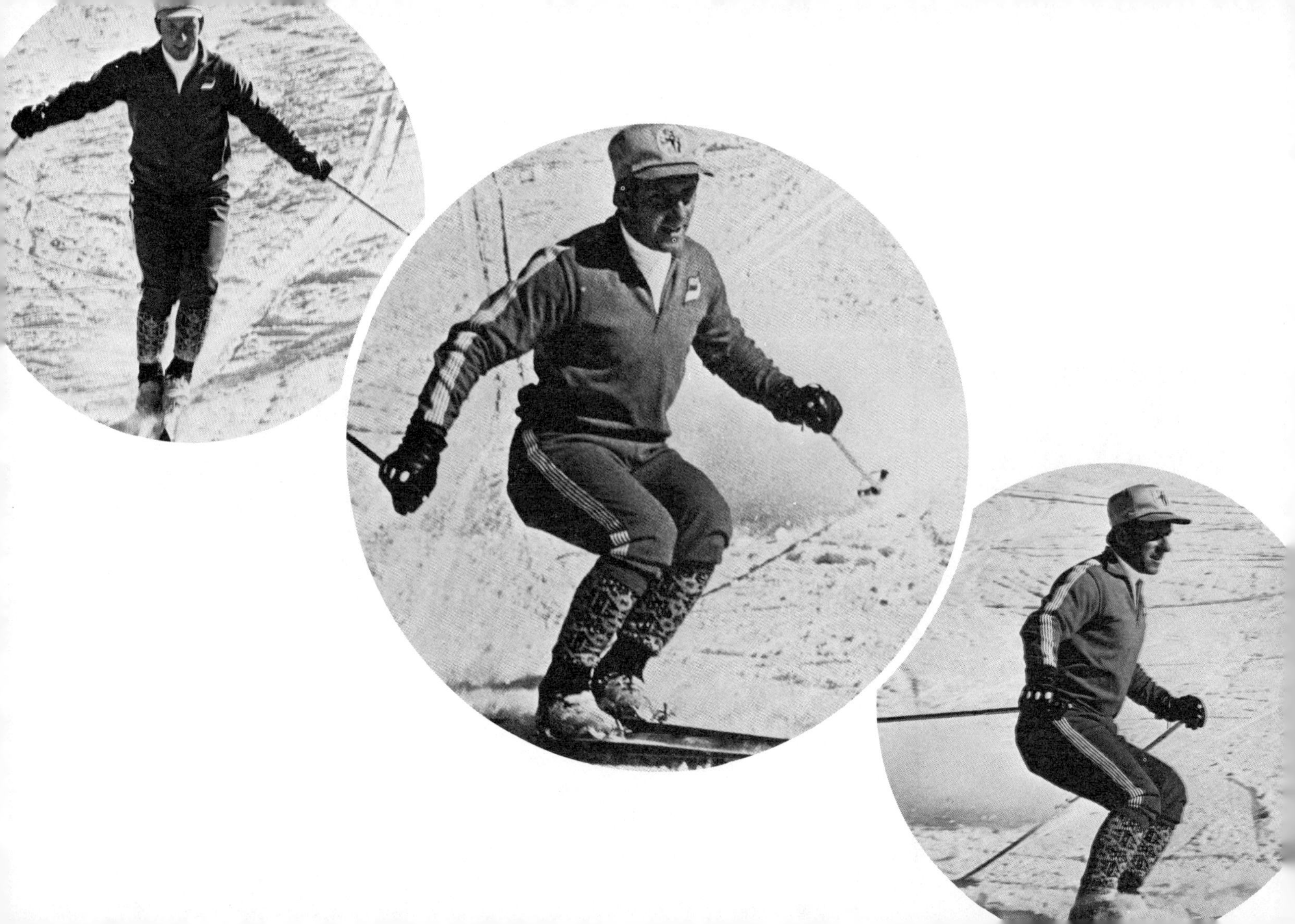

Introduction

Although there are many styles of advanced downhill skiing, touring hasn't as yet adopted any one particular technique. Consequently, any method that works is acceptable. The style easiest for you to master should be used, and most downhill techniques can be applied to the touring situation with only slight modifications.

Because the heel of a touring boot is not fixed to the ski as in downhill skiing, advanced downhill skills require one important adjustment: *your weight must be on the whole foot, with emphasis on the heel*. If you remember this point you should be able to learn most of the downhill turns.

There have been many books written about downhill skiing that cover the variations of basic and advanced turns. I will not dwell on the technical details of the many different styles. I will, however, cover some points of advanced downhill skiing that I have found most useful in ski-touring.

The most advanced turn you have learned so far is the stem turn (see Chapter 3). Turns up to and including the stem turn are commonly known as "steered turns." Now, the progression continues with the stem christie and follows through to the wedeln. In most of these advanced turns a form of unweighting is used, whether it be up-unweighting or down-unweighting. Old-time skiers use the term "swing turn" to describe changes of direction with unweighting.

Unweighting

Unweighting is not new to skiing. It is the release of weight from the skis, which is very helpful in initiating many advanced turns. An exercise to illustrate up-unweighting is jumping up so your skis come off the snow. This can be done either on the flat or when starting a turn. (See next page.)

Down-unweighting can be illustrated best with a bathroom scale. If you stand on the scale and crouch quickly, you will see the pointer swing to a lighter weight for just a moment. The "loss" of weight for that instant is called down-unweighting, and when done on skis, helps to begin a turn. (See facing page.)

139

Edge Control

Edge control, a key ingredient in advanced turns, is accomplished by using the knees and ankles to control the amount of sideslip. You must be able to control a sliding edge for smooth completion of advanced turns.

up-unweighting exercise

Sideslip

Exercises to practice edge control include vertical and forward sideslipping. The sideslip itself is useful when descending steep terrain on a fairly well-packed slope. As an exercise, it should be practiced to be used as part of well-executed parallel turns.

Assume a traverse position on a fairly steep — but short — well-packed hillside. Let the ankles and knees relax, and turn downhill until the skis begin to slip sideways vertically. Roll the ankles and knees uphill to reset the edges and stop the slipping. (It is sometimes easier to work both skis close together as one unit.)

Now, practice the forward sideslip, which is a releasing and slipping of the edges forward and downhill at the same time, on about a forty-five-degree angle to the fall line. To control your direction of slip you can rock your weight a little forward or back.

Try to control various speeds and directions while sideslipping with edge control and weight shift.

Christie Stop

This is the next exercise before we can put the stem christie together. From a downhill traverse, release your edges slightly and then drop down quickly by bending your knees. This will cause a down-unweighting and a turn into the hill. Remember, your knees and ankles can regulate the amount of slipping or edge control you may need. Practice in both directions.

Unweighting Exercise

Ski the fall line at moderate speed in a snowplow position. For a turn to the left, use exaggerated knee bend and point the left ski pole about a foot to the side of the ski tips.

When the pole is planted, up-unweighting should begin. Weight is transferred to the right ski. As the turn is initiated, bring the other ski alongside and resume the normal traverse position.

Stem Christie

You are now ready to practice the next turn in the learning progression, the stem christie, which is similar to the stem turn with these basic additions: use a little more speed, add unweighting, slide the skis together sooner after the stem, and apply edge control with heel thrust (a steady pushing to the outside of the turn with the lower legs).

The stem christie (formerly called the stem christiana) is an old and historical turn. Before fixed-heel bindings, in fact, it was a very advanced turn, while the telemark turn was the one beginners used on gradual slopes with heavy snow.

Apparently, as more skiers packed the snow and fixed-heel bindings (made popular by the Arlberg school of skiing, St. Anton, Austria) became the key to faster downhill trips over the well-packed, bumpy terrain, the telemark turn with the loose-heel apparatus was used less and less.

The stem christie became for the Arlbergers, as they were called, the bridge to the more advanced "swing turns," or "swings," of forty years ago. It might be considered the forerunner of such modern-day parallel skiing skills as the short swing, wedeln, and trick turns, including airplane turns, outriggers, Charlestons, and numerous others.

Despite the prominence of the stem christie in skiing, it became the focal point of heated debates in the 1920s between loose-heel skiers and the Arlbergers.

Arnold Lunn, president of the Ski Club of Great Britain (1928–30), taught the telemark turn to beginners and the stem christie to more advanced skiers while Hannes Schneider, spokesman for the Arlbergers and father of the Arlberg ski technique, argued for leaving the telemark to the experts and concentrating on the stem christie as the most basic turn. Both agreed, however, that downhill turning on steep slopes was best accomplished by the stem christie no matter what kind of binding was used.

Today the stem christie is still an essential turn to know and use, but the telemark turn is used mostly for fun and exhibition skiing. Yet, in a strange turnabout, the loose-heel binding used in ski-touring is becoming popular once again.

The stem christie remains the bridge between the steered turns and parallel skiing. To execute the turn, follow these steps. Remember that with this step-by-step approach, exaggeration may be used to help you "feel" the movement of the new turn. When the technique is mastered, you will be able to execute the movement with confidence, and it won't be necessary to exaggerate any longer.

To execute the turn, begin in a downhill traverse, riding the skis with most of your weight on the downhill ski. Stem the uphill ski and crouch low, using an exaggerated knee bend. Now spring quickly from the downhill ski and transfer your weight to the opposite ski, which becomes your new downhill ski as the turn is completed.

Once your weight has been transferred, bring the unweighted ski up so it is parallel with the other one and resume a moderate knee bend for balance as your skis turn into the fall line.

As your turn continues through its arc, use your knees

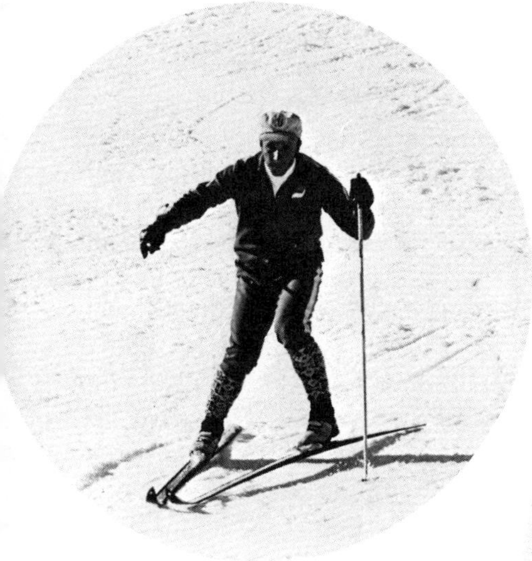
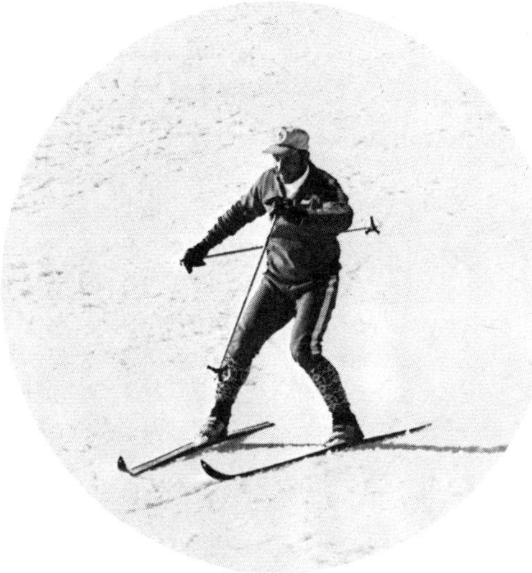
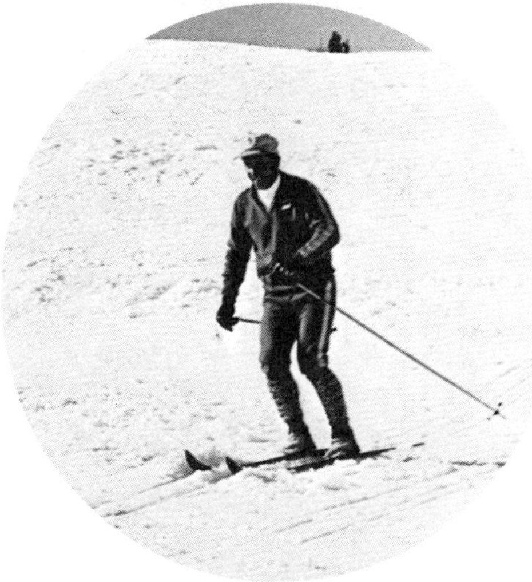
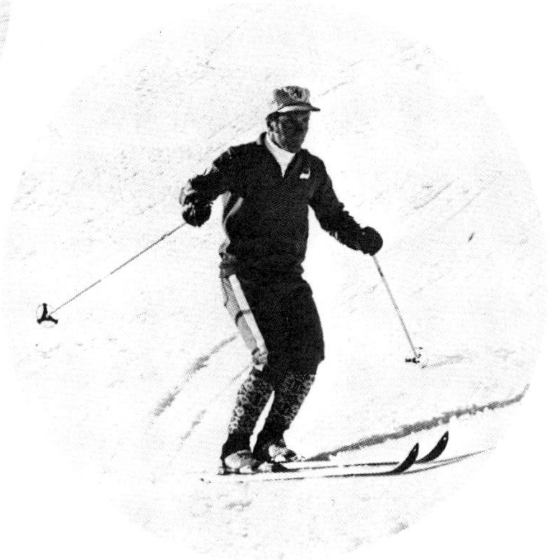
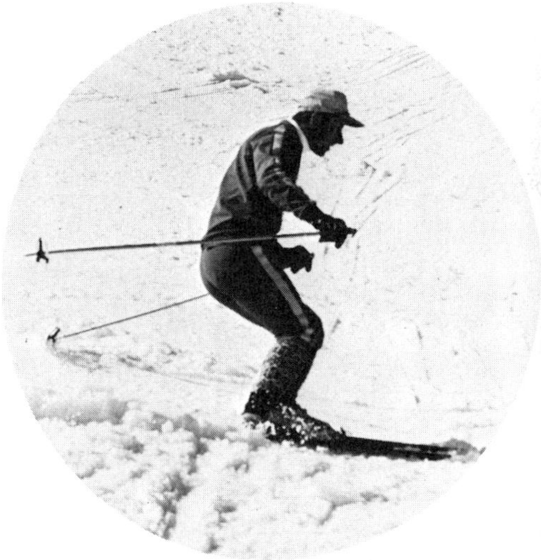

and ankles, along with a little heel thrust, to control the sliding edges for a smooth, complete turn.

OPTIONAL: You may use your ski pole for a timing device and to help you learn weight transfer.

Practice the stem christie in both directions and then link several together. This turn may be used for the steeper hills and slopes in most snow conditions. As you improve, the stem portion of the turn can be reduced and executed more quickly, so more time will be used maintaining a position of sliding parallel skis. When you do this, you will have progressed to advanced ski-touring.

Parallel Christie

By eliminating the stem completely you enter the world of parallel skiing — descending a slope, making turns in both directions with your skis parallel. This is also the prelude to what I consider one of the ultimate experiences in touring: the deep-powder descent.

The key to parallel turns lies in mastering the sensation of skiing a little faster when you execute the new turn.

The parallel christie is initiated from a traverse. First, set the edge of the downhill ski with a down motion. The actual turning begins with an up motion and transfer of weight and edge set to the outside ski (formerly the uphill ski) as it is advanced slightly. The turning process continues with heel thrust to the outside combined with a down or sinking motion and control of the sliding edges until the turn is completed. You will now be traversing in the opposite direction, ready for the next turn. The pole is used in the same manner as in the stem christie: either as a timing device or not at all.

Exercises for Parallel Turning

Pole Plant: Poles can be very useful as a timing device and as an aid for balance. Practice this exercise on level ground first. Assume a straight running position. As you sink to a low knee bend, bring a pole forward. It should be pointed near the tip of the ski and about a foot to the side. Now you are in a position *ready* to unweight the skis and initiate a turn. The signal to begin unweighting is when you plant the pole in the snow. When the right pole is forward, you will turn around it to the right.

Hop into Parallel Skiing: This is one of the better exercises to start with when learning a parallel turn. Actually, all it involves is exaggerated unweighting. Place a pole on each side of you and a little forward. Then, with your skis together, hop from side to side on the level, using your poles only for balance.

Now pick a gentle, well-packed slope. Ski down the fall line, hoping from one side to the other with your skis parallel. In the exercise, it is fine to hop hard enough for the skis to come off the snow.

1

2

3

4

5

6

Ski the Fall Line: Practice the last two exercises together at low speed, using the same gentle, well-packed slope. Exaggerate the hopping with the pole plant. When you feel you have that motion under control, continue to add a little more speed, use less unweighting, and master a more delicate control of your edges. You are now performing a parallel turn. Work on smoothness and rhythm.

When making a parallel turn in more difficult snow conditions, you may have to revert to exaggerated unweighting, edge set and turning effort. But soon you will be able to handle most kinds of terrain with little problem.

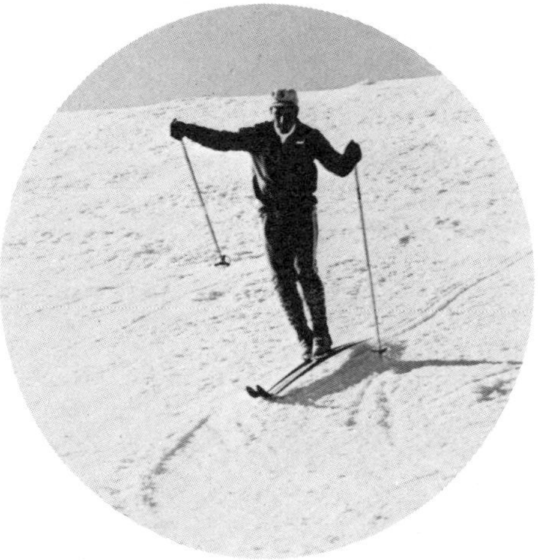
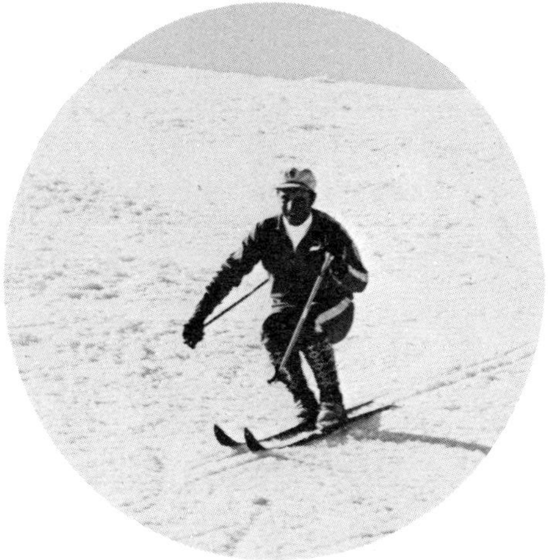
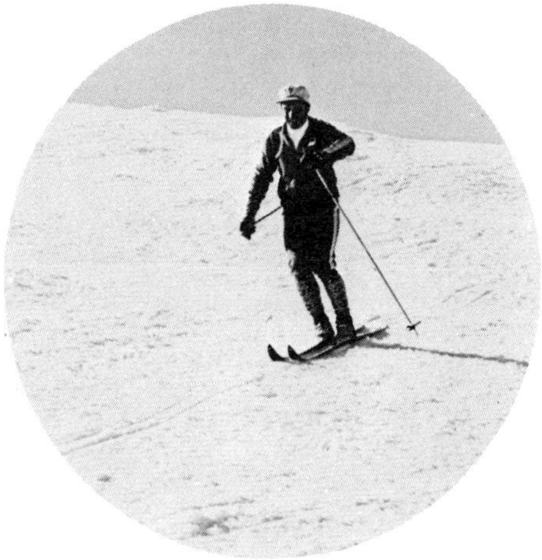
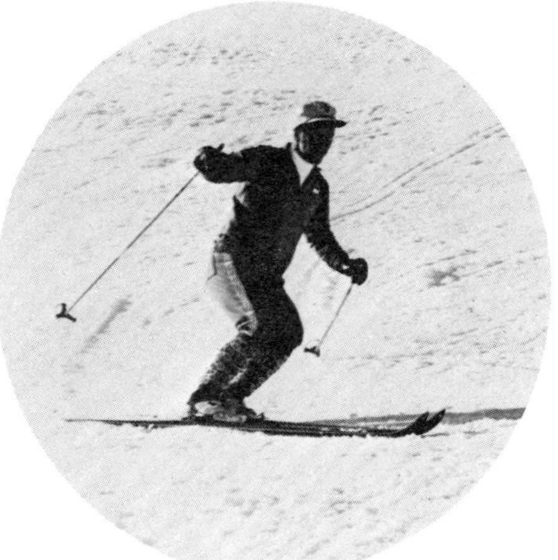
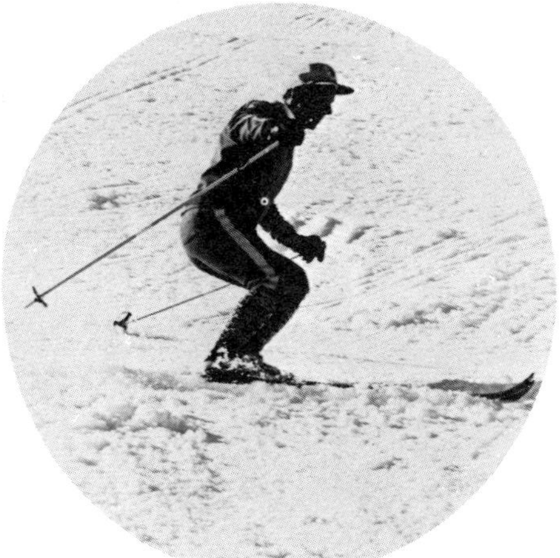
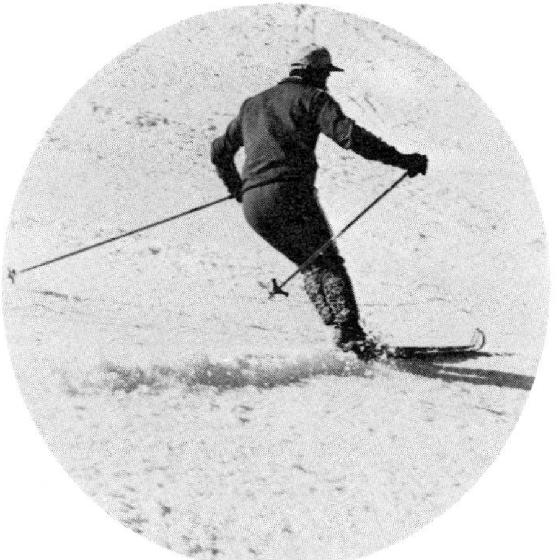

Short Swing

The short swing and wedeln are two of the more popular turns used when skiing downhill in fairly well-packed snow.

The short swing is a form of the parallel christie. Consecutive turns are made down the fall line without traversing, using a definite edge set. To control speed on steep slopes, use a pole plant and a wider turn with more edge set. The steepness of the slope will govern the amount of control necessary. The snow should be fairly well packed.

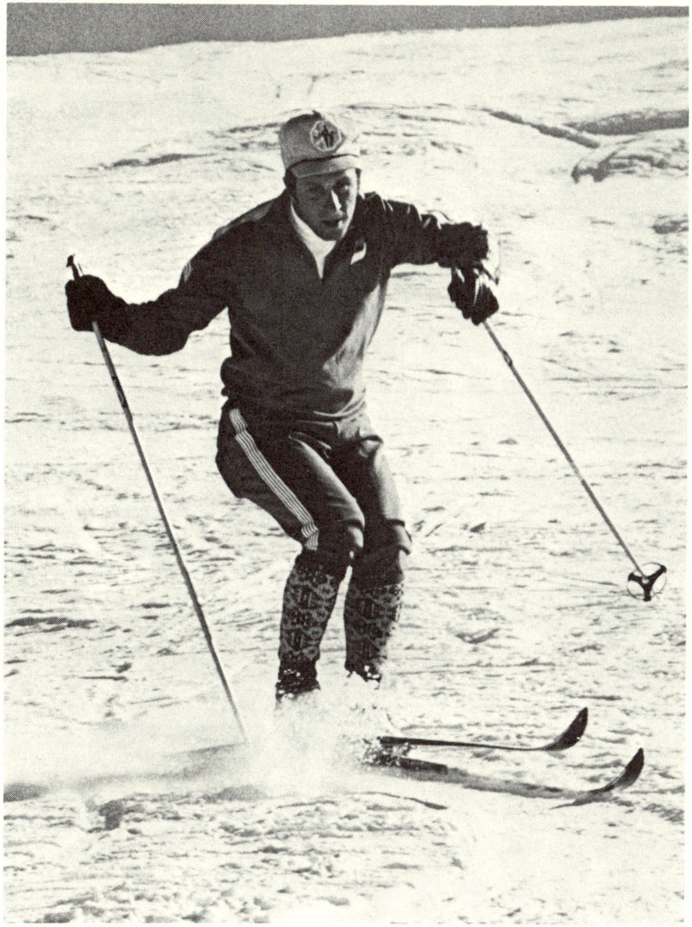

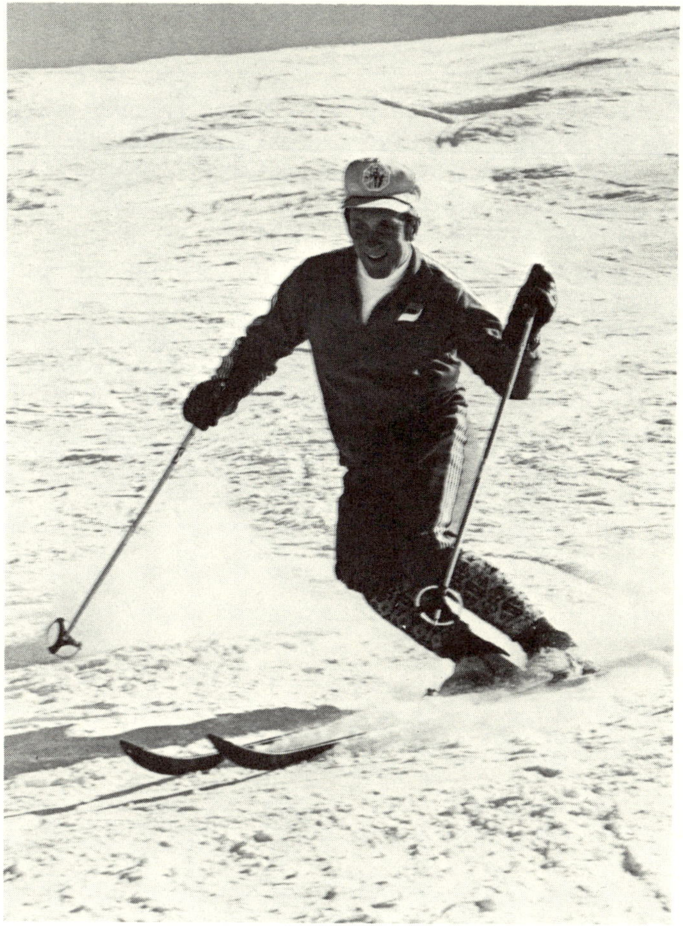

Wedeln

Wedeln is an Austrian word meaning "wiggle" and is used to describe another form of the parallel christie. It is sometimes described as a flowing back and forth of the skis as you descend a hill.

The wedeln is best practiced in the fall line. Make consecutive linked turns without a traverse using very little edge set.

During the linked turns, the skis are kept almost flat with the legs moving back and forth. Very little effort is revealed by the upper body. Smoothness is striven for, and the tracks left in the snow should be serpentine.

Deep-Snow Skills: Skiing the Powder

The motions for a parallel christie, done in a relaxed and exaggerated manner, will lead you to a deep-powder technique.

The keys to powder technique with touring equipment are rhythm, balance and the ability to keep the ski riding on top of the snow, called "ski flotation" or "floating the tips." This will help you to weight both skis equally at all times, which is very important in powder skiing.

Don't be afraid of falling, which happens a lot when learning deep-snow skiing. Here's a hint: when skiing the deep stuff, remember to keep your mouth closed if you begin to fall so you won't inhale any of the dry, light snow into your lungs.

Remember these points for deep-snow skiing:

— Ski in the fall line. Deep snow has a tendency to slow your descent and you need some speed to obtain ski flotation.
— Skis should function as a single unit, otherwise they may track differently. Keep your skis, feet, and legs together.
— Keep your weight over the whole foot with emphasis on the heel.
— Keep skis equally weighted.
— Unweight your skis when turning.
— Have good knee bend. Good knee bend will lower the

center of gravity, providing better balance and a better position to recover from possible falls. Also, a deep-knee bend, in powder skiing and in other kinds of ski-touring, is a good skiing position from which to begin the execution of unweighting.

Also, note that as unweighting begins so does a simultaneous rotation (twisting motion as a turning force) of the upper body in the direction you wish to turn. For the next turn, unweight and rotate in the opposite direction.

After falling in very deep snow, cross your poles to form an "X" to support you as you get up.

Skiing Ice or Hard Pack

During a touring season, you are likely to run into ice or hard-pack snow, especially if you live in the East. If you keep your wits about you as you tour, you can maneuver over these hard spots with less difficulty than a skier who panics.

Ice and hard pack are some of the toughest snow conditions you will encounter on touring skis. There are two basic reasons for this: the lack of stiffness in the touring boot (in contrast to the Alpine boot) to help hold an edge, and the lack of stiffness in the ski, or bottom camber, to provide needed control.

When skiing ice or hard pack, use basically the same techniques as for ordinary snow, but with much less body movement. Very little unweighting and turning force are necessary because of the reduced resistance between ski and snow.

Turn often to keep your speed down, and try to keep the entire ski in contact with the snow. This hint is especially important for the skier without a steel-edged ski.

Don't lean to the inside of the turn! A wooden edge cannot hold a turn, and a steel edge will have trouble. As you begin turning and sliding, be sure you are standing over your skis as much as possible. In other words, slide with the skis, preventing them from slipping out from under you. Use of poles will add extra balance. A metal edge sometimes can hold a turn better than a wooden edge, but usually not enough to really bank it.

The Telemark Turn

A ski-touring book isn't complete without a brief statement about the historical telemark turn, one of the prettiest moves in loose-heel skiing. This is one turn that should be done when the skier has great flexibility in both the boot and the binding. Today, it is performed mostly for exhibition and fun.

The telemark turn is not generally used as a high-speed method of changing direction. It is a steered turn. Practice it on a gradual slope that has a packed base with an inch or two of snow on top for traction. We will try a turn to the right.

Start moving in a straight running position at slow speed. Slide your left ski way forward, turn it slightly right and edge it toward the inside of the turn. Your right ski tip should now be resting near your left ski boot. Most of your weight should be on the forward ski. The trailing ski acts as a stabilizer and helps you maintain balance.

Practice the telemark turn in both directions and then try to link them. You are doing what skiers did fifty to a hundred years ago.

Many other special tricks can be done on touring skis, such as jumps and royal christies. You should never feel you have reached the top and there is nothing more to learn.

Touring combines the best of two worlds: overland journeys to peaceful hideaways and the thrill and excitement of

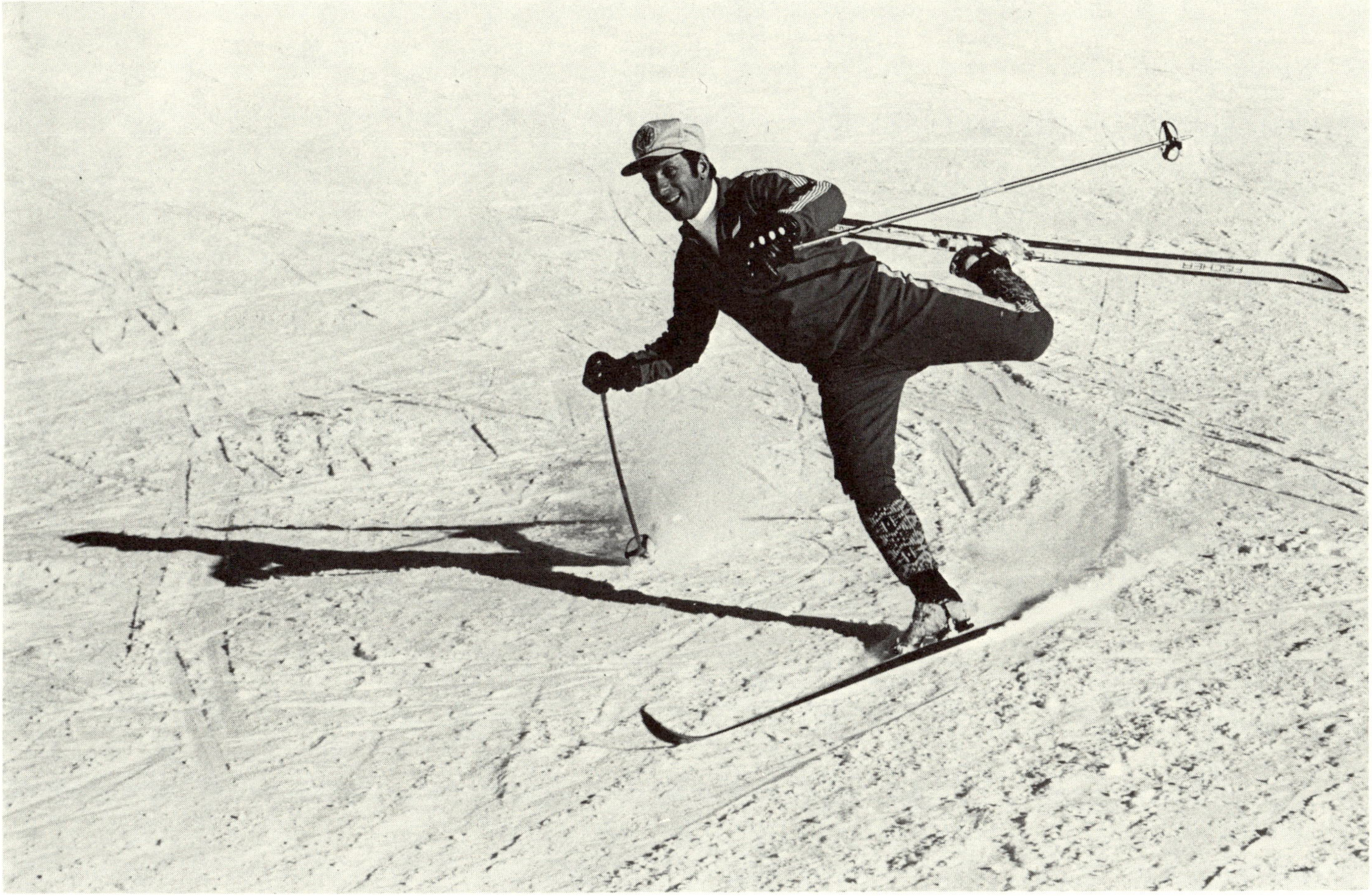

downhill skiing. To get the best of both worlds and to prevent some bad habits that will be hard for you to change, try to obtain some good, qualified instruction first, then go practice.

Remember, ski-touring is just for the fun of it!

7 | The Overnight Tour

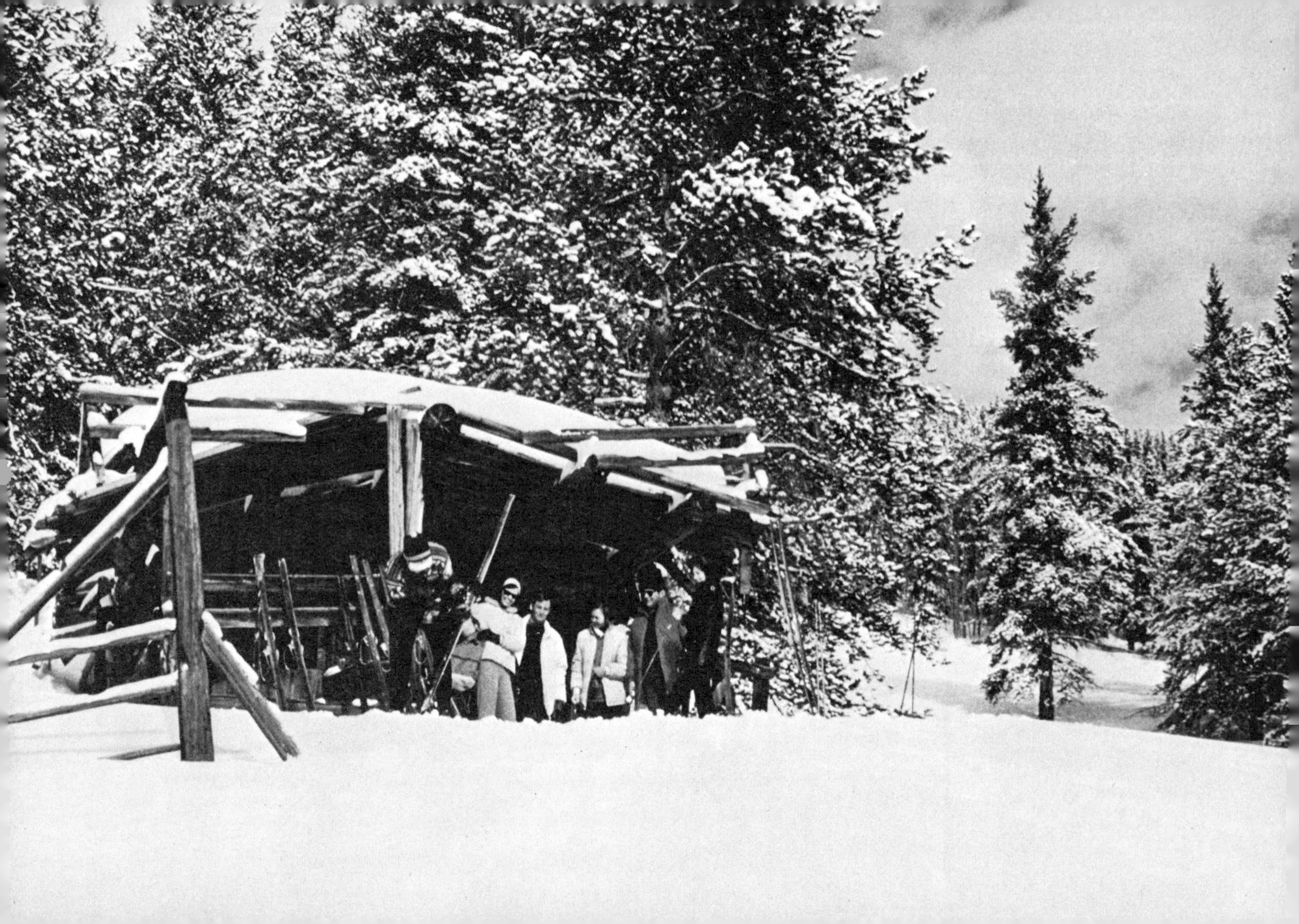

What Is an Overnight?

One of the more adventurous aspects of ski-touring is the extended trip, or the overnight, when skiers trek for more than one day and spend a night or so in a hut or winter camp.

Even if you never plan to go on an overnight tour, some knowledge of winter camping is necessary for emergency situations. Storms can blow up unexpectedly, and you might be forced to dig in.

Snow can be used to your advantage in bad weather conditions. Animals and birds burrow into the snow and survive, and man can, too. Snow caves, trenches, or even hollows beneath pine trees can provide cover if you get caught in the backcountry. Government snow surveyors are routinely taught how to hole up in snow when the weather turns bad, for they travel in very remote areas.

Besides learning how to adapt to the winter environment, snow surveyors are taught two other important principles that apply to all outdoor activity — keep your energy level high and don't panic if something goes wrong.

Of course, that is easy to say but hard to do if you are the one suddenly caught in a blizzard. A little knowledge can take you a long way, however. Knowing what to do is important.

This is where a good leader really pays off. He will be able to delegate authority and make decisions that will benefit everyone. Arguing and debating is exhausting and takes time that could be used better elsewhere.

When going on an overnight for the first time, have a good leader. You will be able to learn some of the finer points of winter camping from him.

There are several kinds of overnight tours. Touring to a mountain cabin is something to look forward to, especially if the shelter has cooking utensils, bunks and a wood-burning stove. Such huts exist and can be found by writing touring centers or the United States Ski Association (see Appendix).

State and federal park officials, mountain clubs and outdoor groups can be good sources of information on places to camp, whether you use tents, abandoned cabins, or touring huts. Such organizations might also have valuable information on weather, snow conditions and skier density. You don't want to overcrowd any one area. Twenty people in a five-man hut could be too cozy. Be sure to let somebody know where you are going and when you will be back. Then, if something happens, people will know where to look.

For the overnight trip, add a sleeping bag and more food to the day pack, and you should have enough gear to be comfortable.

Equipment

With the right equipment, camping in the snow can be quite pleasant and is often more exciting than staying in a cabin. Modern technology has produced easy-to-carry, lightweight gear that will keep you snug in most weather conditions.

Since you will be adding more weight to your day pack, it is essential that your carrier for the overnight be well built and properly fitted. There are numerous packs for touring, but a good frame and comfortable sack are necessary. A poorly constructed, badly fitting backpack can make a trip miserable. Generally, good packs will run from thirty-five to seventy-five dollars. I recommend a frame and sack combination that can distribute the weight on the hips for lower center of gravity while skiing.

In addition to the day-pack supplies you might take:

— A canteen with water. Keeping up the water content of the body is important.

— A good supply of matches, and possibly, a portable gas stove. Lightweight and functional stoves (around ten dollars) are available and can really make a difference if firewood is hard to come by, or if you want a quick cup of coffee but don't want to build a fire.

— A small saw or hatchet (about three dollars).

— Sleeping bag and ensolite pad or air mattress. Ensolite is a closed-cell foam pad that will not soak up moisture and can be used on the snow under your sleeping bag or as a warm, dry seat cushion. Even a pad only a half-inch thick can provide plenty of insulation under you. Air mattresses aren't as good, in my estimation. They have a tendency to leak and conduct cold more easily.

Get a good sleeping bag that has been tested to low temperatures. The sleeping bag is an extremely important piece of equipment and could save your life. Don't go into winter woods with a bag that would be fine for a warm summer evening but is marginal in a winter camp. There are several warm, lightweight bags, some with removable liners that can be taken out for easy cleaning, that can be pushed into a stuff sack for easy packaging and carrying. They cost anywhere from sixty to more than one hundred dollars.

— Food for all meals plus one extra portion. There are numerous good dried and freeze-dried foods on the market. Trail Chef has a variety of dishes that would make the sourdough boys drool. Remember, the food should be lightweight and high in energy. When planning for food, keep in mind you will eat more out skiing then you ordinarily do at home. The extra portion is in case you must spend a longer time touring then you expected.

— Cooking equipment. Pots and pans that nest and fit into one neat package are terrific for camping. These can be lightweight and most have enough room between clustered pots and multiple pan lids for eating utensils, spices, and dish cleaners. Remember, not everyone in the party has to carry a pot and a pan. Try and figure out how many cooking items will be needed at mealtime and then divide up the weight. If one person carries cooking gear, another should carry a little more food. Divide the weight among the group so no one person is overburdened.

Sometimes, small, portable wire grills come in handy, especially to rest a pot or pan over a fire.

— A repair kit is important. At least one member of the group should carry extra parts for skis, bindings, and backpacks, plus assorted screws and bolts and combination tools.

— A lightweight shovel (some have detachable handles for easy backpacking) has many uses, especially when digging a snow cave or snow trench.

— Extra clothing, such as cotton socks, T-shirt and wool shirt, will provide a dry change after a day on the trail. I have found afterski boots or knee-high mucklucks a godsend after a full day on touring skis.

Campsites

Where you want to spend the night in the woods is up to you, but here are several hints that should help you pick a good campsite and build a safe, comfortable camp.

— There should be a good supply of burnable wood nearby, a stand of trees for shelter, and a place to catch the morning sun. The site should be close to water for drinking and cooking. It is possible to melt snow for liquid, but this takes a long time and consumes plenty of fuel.
— Springs and streams are a good source of water. If you don't know whether the water is good or bad, purify it by boiling or using a purifying agent, which can be purchased in pill form at most sporting-goods stores.
— If you build a fire, keep it away from tents, sleeping bags, or any material made of nylon, because wind-blown sparks can burn them full of holes.
— The posh snow camp has paths dug from sleeping areas to a central campfire. This can be done by packing the snow with skis or shoveling. A shoveled path is more efficient, but it isn't necessary. A good trail system can eliminate struggling around in waist-deep snow.
— Keeping your gear dry is very important. Some items can be hung on trees so they are off the snow and out of the way of hungry animals. Other equipment can be placed on wood platforms.

— To make camp takes an hour or longer, so plan your day's travel accordingly. Leave plenty of time at the end of skiing to put up camp in daylight. Making camp in the dark is not only difficult but can also be wet and cold.

If you ski until dusk, you are asking for trouble, for as soon as the sun sets the temperature will quickly drop. After a long day of skiing you should be comfortably tired, not exhausted. If you haven't saved a little energy to establish a camp, bedding down for the night will be a chore, better yet, plain drudgery. The frivolity that should surround a campfire will be nothing more than chowing down for an uncomfortable night. An exasperating night in an ill-chosen campsite could make the next day's journey a long one. But a good night's sleep will prepare you for a fun day of skiing.

Shelters

Lean-to: There are three basic winter-camping shelters skiers use on overnights: a snow cave, a snow trench, and a tent. The familiar lean-to, popular years ago, has fallen from favor because of the ecology movement to save trees. But if you are caught in the backcountry without a shovel or tent, you might have to build a lean-to.

The lean-to is basically a roof and windbreak to protect a sleeping area. It consists of two vertical support poles (separated a few feet) topped by a horizontal beam. Logs are then leaned against the horizontal piece at an angle, making a steep, pitched roof. The finished product should resemble a soccer goal. Brush can be used to cover the structure, and snow can be placed over the roof and sides for more protection.

Try to construct the lean-to with old logs and dead brush and cover with a ground cloth (such as a space blanket). Use live trees and pine boughs only in case of emergency. If snow is used without a tarp, be careful it doesn't melt and soak the equipment inside.

A ground cover and rope can also be used to build a lean-to. Tie the rope between two trees and drape the material over it. Use snow and/or logs and rocks to secure the tarp at the bottom.

Snow Cave and Snow Trench: There is a familiar play on words around ski areas when things get out of hand.

167

Managers and employees look at each other and say, "It's snow use," meaning it's time to give up. But such a pun has a different meaning in the backcountry, where snow can be used to great advantage. Six inches of snow can provide good insulation, and you can make a nice home away from home by digging into the white stuff. A classic example of a snow house is an Eskimo igloo.

A snow cave or snow trench provides good protection from the elements and allows body heat to warm the enclosure. Caves are warmer than trenches but take longer to build and are more difficult to construct. If you don't have a shovel, you can survive cold nights by crawling into dry spaces beneath snow-draped pines and spruces.

A snow cave can be a palace or a cubbyhole. Some very ingenious "caves" are dug by architecture students from Montana State University in Bozeman. Each winter the students construct a snow shelter and cook dinner for the faculty. Time limit: one day.

What the students have been able to build is impressive. One group dug out a room with a domed ceiling. A circular bench was sculpted into the wall opposite the entrance, which was a curving snow slide. The students sat on the bench and called to the teachers to enter. One by one, each member of the faculty slid belly-first into the room and took his place on the bench. When all had entered, a six-course meal was served. The wine was chilled in the snow.

Less glamorous, and at the opposite end of the size spectrum, lies the one-man berth, a snug two feet by two feet by eight feet, which can easily be dug.

A good-sized dwelling takes several strong diggers a few hours to complete but can last up to a week before the roof begins to sag. A one-night stand isn't worth the effort to build a multiperson cave. But if you are going to do several days of camping and skiing in one location it might be worthwhile.

Caves should be dug in deep drifts free from avalanche danger. The snow should be packed solid by wind and sun. Dig a tunnel into the bank about three feet high and wide and away from the prevailing wind direction. The entrance should slope gently upward so snow from the outside won't blow in overnight. The floor of the cave should be above the tunnel entrance to keep the cold air from coming in. The roof should be at least six inches thick.

For a small cave, make the living area only as large as necessary for skiers and equipment (not including skis or poles). The ceiling should be domed for support and to drain water to the sides. It should be kept low to better maintain heat from body temperature and cookstove.

After you have been in the cave a while, a slight melting of the ceiling will take place, leaving a refrozen ice glaze throughout the interior that will greatly strengthen the cave.

You must remember to have ventilation, either from the entrance and/or a hole in the roof. In smaller caves you should be able to poke a ski pole through the roof for air.

When digging a big cave, the entrance should be quite large and run about ten feet into the drift to a central chamber of standing height. Sleeping rooms can branch off the main hall. You should level them off about knee height so you can have a place to sit. Shelves for sleeping can be up to four feet high and nine feet long. This will allow good sleeping comfort. To build a cave like this takes a lot of time and hard work.

Portable gas stoves and candles are good for heating and lighting caves. The temperature inside can be a comfortable twenty to twenty-eight degrees when the outside temperature is subzero.

A trench shelter is easier to make than a snow cave and can be just as nice. A big plus with trenches is that you can lie in your sleeping bag and look at the stars.

A trench is really a "grave" dug about two feet deep in the snow. The bottom of the pit should be covered first with dry, dead twigs and then a ground cover. A foam pad or air mattress can be placed on top of the floor. For added protection, the top of the trench can be covered with dead logs, an extra tarp and a little snow.

Tents: The tent is the most versatile shelter because you don't have to rely on snow depth, a shovel, or dead logs and bushes. You can usually erect a tent in places where a snow cave cannot be made. Lightweight, compact, and easy-to-carry tents are readily available. Modern designs make pitching a tent simple, and you don't have to cut down living trees for support. An ensolite pad will make a good floor. I prefer a tent with a tunnel opening for winter camping, and drawstrings are better than zippers, which have a tendency to freeze up in really cold weather. Good tents can cost from seventy to more than one hundred dollars.

Fires

There is nothing like a campfire to bring out the goodness in people. And the most ordinary food cooked over an open blaze will taste as if it came from the kitchen of a professional chef. After an exhilarating tour through the woods and having prepared your camp for the night, you will be ready to enjoy the best that winter camping has to offer. A well-fed skier warmed by a fire is likely to get a new lease on life.

You will need to build a platform on the snow for your fire until coals are developed. Or, if possible, dig a pit to ground level and then start your fire. The pit should be large enough for a person to attend to the cooking.

Begin with dried twigs from dead logs or branches of trees. Gather wood on skis. It is easier than trudging through the snow on foot. The flames should heat the inside of the hole. If the snow melts, it will only enlarge the pit sufficiently to refreeze. Then you can sit at the edge of the cavity, your feet warmed by the fire.

When the only available wood is wet, try the steel-wool trick to start your fire. Take a small pinch of fine steel wool and put a few small branches on it. Add to that combination a little larger kindling. Light a candle and put it to the steel wool. Blow lightly on the flame and the fire should start. Steel wool can also be used for removing wax and for scouring pots and pans.

You can use your ensolite pad or space blanket to sit on.

If you use your skis or a log as a seat, put an extra hat or pair of gloves on top of them. This will keep your knickers warm and dry while sitting down.

If you don't have a grill, you can suspend pots over the fire by avalanche cord or other rope tied between two trees. Aluminum foil can be used in place of a pan if you desire.

Soap-impregnated scouring pads can be used for cleanup. Eating from greasy utensils can make you sick, so cleaning them is a good idea.

The Menu

You will need at least four meals for an overnight tour. A sample menu might be something like this:

Breakfast: Coffee or tea, oatmeal, granola and/or powdered eggs, bread, and dehydrated juice, such as Tang or Wyler's.

Lunch: Sandwich meats or sausage, cheese, and/or soup, dried fruit, juice, tea or coffee, candy or nuts. If you have oranges, two things can be done. First, cut a hole in the top of the orange, put some sugar in the opening, squeeze the fruit, and drink the mixture. Next, peel and eat the orange. Save the peels and put them in your canteen. This makes the liquid slightly acidic and is a better thirst quencher than plain water.

NOTE: Drink plenty of water, even on a cold day. This will help to prevent dehydration, which is important.

Dinner: Soup, freeze-dried dinner, vegetables, dessert (candy), coffee, tea, or hot chocolate.

For extra energy along the trail, a mixture of M&M's, nuts, raisins, and coconut — called "gorp" — can be carried in a plastic Baggie. It makes good nibbling.

An extra lunch is probably a good idea, just in case you stay longer than you plan.

Map and Compass Skills

When touring, it is important to know where you are at all times. Knowing how to use a map and compass can help you pinpoint your position.

There are several good books on map reading and compass use. One of the best is Björn Kjellstrom's *Be Expert with Map and Compass.* For determining position with map and compass, Kjellstrom coined the word "orienteering."

In the United States there is an orienteering championship. This little-known contest pits man, compass and map against flags placed over a course. Given the flag positions on a map, the person who can find the checkpoints on land quickest and reach the finish line is the winner.

Orienteering contests can also be held on skis, but to prevent the first person's tracks being followed, each contestant is given different checkpoints to locate.

Apart from the fun, learning to use a compass and map can prevent you from becoming lost, or if lost, can help you find your way home. Below are a few rules from the Ski-Touring Certification Committee of the Rocky Mountain Division of the United States Ski Association designed to acquaint you with orienteering.

Orienteering Terms: *True North (or South)* is the point where the earth's rotational axis intersects its surface. Most geographic maps are oriented with respect to true north.

Magnetic North is the point on the earth to which all

171

magnetic compasses point. Magnetic north is approximately twelve hundred miles below true north, so a needle pointing toward magnetic north is not necessarily pointing toward true north. As a matter of fact, magnetic north, as indicated by a compass needle, only points to true north when they are in line. Such a place could be on the Great Lakes or on the west edge of Hudson Bay.

If you move west of an imaginary line that passes through true north and magnetic north, your compass will point east of true north, as the needle aligns itself with magnetic north. This is called "easterly variation."

If you move east of the imaginary line, your compass needle will point west of true north, and this is called "westerly variation."

A Bearing is a horizontal angle fixing a direction with respect to direction north that signifies a straight line of travel.

Map Bearing is a bearing from one point to another fixed on a map with direction north marked by grid lines, or meridians.

Field Bearing is a bearing from one point to another where direction north is pointed out by a magnetic needle.

Map Bearing Rules: To set a bearing, turn the degree dial of the compass until the bearing you desire is shown on the bearing pointer. To set your compass to a bearing of sixty, for example, turn the degree dial until the number sixty appears on the bearing pointer.

To face the bearing you have set on your compass, hold the compass level in your hand, permitting the magnetic needle to swing freely, and have the bearing indicator pointing straight ahead. Turn yourself, together with the compass, until the north end of the magnetic needle points to the letter "N" on the degree dial.

Looking now in the direction of the bearing pointer, you are facing a bearing of sixty. To walk or follow this bearing, look straight ahead (the farther the better) and choose a landmark or spot that is in the direction you are facing, as indicated by the direction of the travel arrow on the compass. When you get there, use the compass to locate the next landmark in the bearing of sixty degrees and repeat the procedure until you reach your destination.

Field Bearing Rules: To take a field bearing, simply work from terrain to map as follows: Face the landmark (hill, buildings or whatever) on which you intend to take a bearing, either to plot on your map or to give you a course to follow. Hold your compass with the bearing pointer directed at the actual landmark and level enough to permit the needle to swing freely. Turn the degree dial, without changing the position of the whole compass, until the N on the dial coincides with the magnetic needle (red end).

Now you can read on the dial at the bearing pointer the magnetic bearing to the actual landmark.

Adjusting for Variation: You might have to take into consideration the variation between true north and magnetic north. In California, magnetic north varies, or is declined, from fifteen to twenty degrees east of true north. Adjusting for variation is known on most maps as "declination."

If you have a map that doesn't indicate a declination, you can find true north from the North Star (which rests in the sky above the North Pole), and then using your compass easily figure the variation.

If your compass doesn't have a luminous dial, or you can't see your compass needle at night, then set up a north-south axis by aligning two sticks with the North Star. In the morning you will be able to figure the approximate variation from the north-south line.

Be sure you are reading your compass correctly. On some compasses, south is easily mistaken for north.

Maps: Probably the best maps for the general touring skier are the United States Geological Survey (USGS) topographic fifteen-minute quadrangle maps. These are sometimes called "topo maps" or "quad maps." One map covers a local area fifteen minutes in latitude by fifteen minutes in longitude, and shows natural and most man-made features at the time of survey. The scale is usually one inch equals one mile.

Topo maps define terrain by means of contour lines that follow equal elevations and a color code: solid green, timber; green dots, brush; and white space, open areas such as meadows. However, these areas of vegetation are only approximate, due either to new growths or the harvesting of natural resources.

The distance between contour lines represents a slope, usually a distance of forty to eighty feet in the mountains. This means that a thirty-foot cliff might not show on the map. The closer together the contour lines, the steeper the slope.

These USGS maps can be purchased from local sporting-goods stores. If one shop doesn't have the maps, employees can usually tell you where to find them. They cost about a dollar.

When purchasing a topo map, you might want to tell the shopkeeper you are going to travel in a particular area, and he should know the best map for you. However, you can order the maps for areas of the country east of the Mississippi River directly from the USGS, 1200 South East Street, Arlington, Virginia, 22202. For areas west of the Mississippi write USGS, Denver Federal Center, Lakewood, Colorado, 80215.

Care of the Woods

Please don't litter in the woods or backcountry. Snow is a bad place to hide trash, because when it melts, the refuse will be visible.

Burn the paper items, and if you pack in tin goods or glass containers, carry them out. Some areas have trash cans. Use them.

Everything carried in and not consumed should be carried out. Keep the woods beautiful and unspoiled for the next person or for yourself the next year.

If you are staying in a hut and wood is cut for your use, be sure to replace it for the next tired arrival. Leaving canned goods in a cabin is a nice gesture.

The backcountry is there to be used unless we damage it beyond repair. The more damage, the more regulations will be placed on both winter and summer campers. Please take care of what we have.

Don't Rush the Overnight

Before heading out on a two-day trip, take several one-day tours. Be sure you know how to use and repair your equipment. Test your gear before you are in the backcountry and discover your sleeping-bag zipper doesn't work. Build up to the overnight, making sure you are in good health and physical shape. Then you will enjoy winter camping.

8 | The Four-Day Touring Trek

Cortlandt Freeman, ready to go.

Introduction

The long tour, a three-or-more-day journey into the hidden recesses of the wilderness, is the ultimate in ski-touring. Such a trip can change your life.

There are easy and hard long tours, the main difference being the terrain covered. Overnight trips on established routes with sleeping huts along the way are easier than new-trail journeys over mountains and hills with many nights of winter camping.

Long tours are an adventure, a turning back of the clock to a time when man and nature worked together. Several days on a touring trek give a person a chance to function with and within his environment, to become aware of the forces of nature and to learn to respect them.

In midwinter 1970 I helped head up a four-day tour over seventy-five miles of snowbound wilderness between Vail and Aspen, Colorado, an area of towering mountains that sees little of man, even summer hikers.

Planning

An immense amount of study and preparation was needed to pioneer the new trail, and a measure of success or failure rested in our advance planning, because we would be off the beaten track, where normal assistance in emergency situations wasn't available.

First, each of the twelve men going had to be in excellent physical condition and have plenty of competence on touring skis.

Second, we had to decide on an exact route, making daily goals reasonable.

Third, we had to obtain and test the gear we would take, make lists of clothing and food, and put it all together.

Fourth, we had to notify the Forest Service and ski patrols, obtain clearance, and have a backup force ready in case of trouble. In many respects, planning a four-day tour is similar to filing an airplane flight plan: you designate your departure and arrival time, and your route. If something goes wrong, then, rescuers know where to look.

The idea in any such trip is to plan for unexpected complications, the unknowns in any adventure. Testing gear in practice tours is one way to prevent mishaps later. Getting up-to-date information from reliable sources on weather and snow conditions for the area to be crossed is another way to hedge against disaster and prevent failure. Little items count, too. For example, on a long tour somebody in the group should carry extra backpack parts, especially the pins that hold the pack straps to the frame. Carrying a broken pack can wear you out.

Part of the preparation for the Vail-Aspen tour involved studying stereoscopic maps (three-dimensional photos of terrain) belonging to the Forest Service. (The Forest Service became one of our main sources of information, and they proved to be reliable and good.) We used the stereoscopic maps to decide the best way to approach the highest part of our trip — a major range of the Colorado Rockies that separates Vail and Aspen.

Two approaches were considered: one across a frozen lake, Homestake Reservoir; the other up a wide creek drainage. Following creeks is often a good way to travel in the mountains, but we had to be wary of narrow gullies with steep open slopes on either side, for they are potential avalanche hazards.

The reservoir had drawbacks too, for it had steep avalanche chutes vaulting upwards from two shores. Since the lake was wide in parts and completely frozen, we could weave across the ice, avoiding direct snowslide paths but running a gauntlet, nevertheless.

The drainage looked safer on the maps, but the creek path ended in three, stubby fingers of rock that looked menacing through the stereoscope. Avalanche danger or rock-climbing, those seemed to be our choices.

Winter rock work with full pack, including skis, is difficult, but we had to balance the difficulty against the danger of snowslides. If we couldn't get over the cliffs (presuming we took the drainage first), then we would have to back around and tackle the snow chutes while traversing the frozen reservoir.

The choice had little effect on one member of the tour, Karl Hoechtl, a Vail ski instructor from Austria, recipient of the highest ski-instructor certificate in his native country.

Karl just nodded his head when presented with the alternatives. Yes, we can avoid avalanches, and yes, the pinnacles would be all right. He rolled his shoulders like a prizefighter.

"Maybe we get some tough mountaineering in there, ya?" A faint gleam lighted his blue eyes.

"I get thadt far, I don't turn back for no pinnacles. I crawl over dem."

We decided to fly over the terrain the day before we left on the tour and check on the amount of snow along each route. After the flight, the lake course and its drainage (Homestake Creek), was chosen.

The planning effort consisted of studying the country to be crossed, giving suggestions, discussing alternative plans, checking weather reports, consulting with the Forest Service and other experts, notifying the proper officials, and writing an approximate itinerary. If the trail had been well known, planning would have been easier because the Forest Service probably would have had all the information.

The Pack

Weight is very important on long tours, and it is smart not to carry too much. Being bogged down with unessential items, like a big lantern when a flashlight will do, is asking for trouble. A long-tour list should run something like this, but changes or additions can be made to take into consideration the part of the country where the touring will be done.

— Three pair wool socks
— Two pair long underwear
— One wool sweater
— Wind parka
— Face mask
— Wool hat with ear protection
— Two pair gloves or mittens
— One pair mitten shells
— One pair goggles or dark glasses
— Watch
— ChapStick and/or glacier cream
— Personal toilet articles
— Personal first aid
— Diarrhea pills and vitamins
— Touring skis, poles, bindings
— Extra ski tip
— Spare binding parts, including an assortment of screws
— Ski waxes, scraper and cork
— Pack sack and frame
— Three waterproof stuff sacks, approximately 9" x 11"
— Sleeping bag with waterproof stuff sack
— Ensolite sleeping pad
— Lightweight tent (can be omitted if snow caves or other shelters are to be used)
— Lightweight gas stove and extra gas
— Box of matches
— Food (dehydrated for lightness and compactness)
— Set of eating utensils
— Metal cup, saucepan or small pot
— One quart widemouthed water bottle
— Paper toweling
— Plastic bags
— Flashlight or head lamp
— Jackknife or Swiss Army knife
— Extra backpack parts
— Pliers, screwdriver, small amount of wire
— Lightweight shovel, aluminum with detachable handle
— Small saw
— Maps, compass, pencil and paper
— One hundred feet of brightly colored avalanche cord

On our tour, each man ended up packing about forty pounds.

On a long tour, certain items can be taken or omitted according to personal preference. This list is only a guide, and if cabins or shelters are available, it can be greatly reduced, especially if the huts are supplied with pots and pans, axes and bunks. With the increased popularity of touring, more huts will become available for winter travel.

Someone has suggested tepees for the use of skiers be set up in the fall along touring routes and taken down in the spring. This would be helpful, for the less you have to pack, the better off you will be.

The Trip

The twelve of us met in Vail the night before the expedition. We checked our gear, made sure our equipment was in perfect condition, put a good base of pine tar on our skis, parceled out food, packed backpacks, and then relaxed. We went to bed early.

It was fifteen degrees below zero Friday morning at the top of ten-thousand-plus-foot Vail Pass, starting point for the four-day trek. Greetings were brief in the frosty morning, still dark — an ink-black sky and a billion stars pinpointing infinite distance.

The forty-pound backpacks felt especially heavy. Some picked theirs up, tried them on, and then took them off, wondering if anything could be left behind.

Narrow touring skis with loose heel bindings were readied, backpacks adjusted, poles gathered. With the first faint rays of the morning sun, we shoved off. The sun was only a scratch of light on mountaintops, lifting the canopy of the night and slowly changing the sky to a heavy blue — a color you could almost swim through.

From Vail Pass, we would climb south to Shrine Pass, a rise of seven hundred feet in three miles and then, following Turkey Creek, would descend to the little town of Redcliff (altitude, eighty-six hundred feet) jammed into a mountain ravine.

From there we would turn west, climb along Homestake Creek just below the continental divide to an altitude of

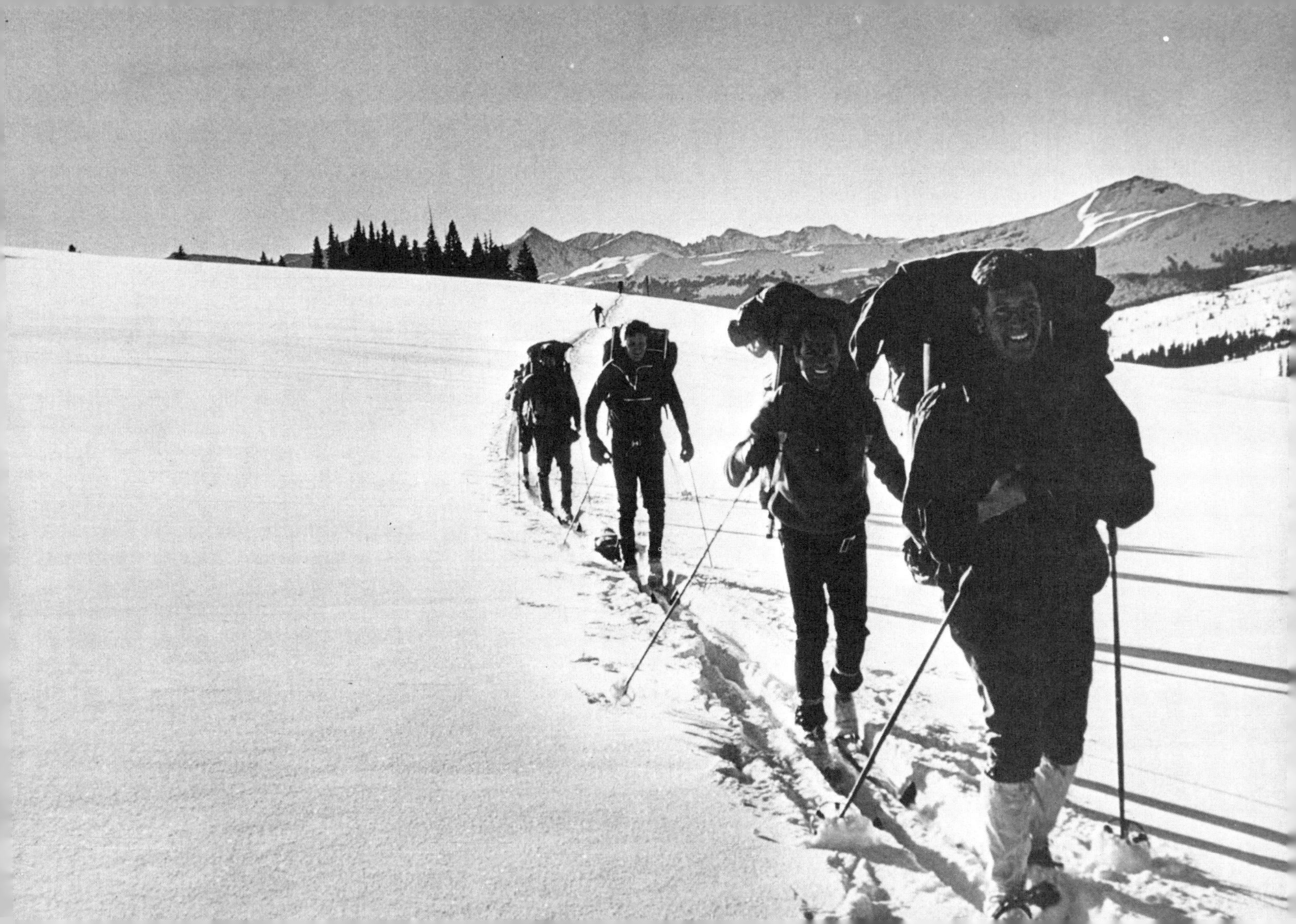

twelve thousand, seven hundred feet, and then take a long, downhill run to the upper reaches of the Frying Pan River. We would climb out of that drainage to the top of Mt. Porphyry, ski into the upper Woody Creek drainage, ascend the backside of Red Mountain, and then join Hunter Creek for the final leg into Aspen.

The climb to Shrine Pass warmed us. We peeled off a layer of clothing and were skiing in sweaters and wind parkas before cresting the pass. And the sun was full upon us.

The descent along Turkey Creek was swift and easy. Weathered stumps, possibly from older logging days, or perhaps a silent reminder of Indian wars or man's folly with fire, protruded through sculptured mounds of snow, while bursts of sunlight knifed between thick forests of evergreens. The higher mountains twisted away to the horizon — some blown bare of snow, others draped in winter's white cloak.

We slid into Redcliff to the amazed stares of its residents. Our plan had been to eat breakfast there, and we were hungry.

Bacon, sausage, eggs, and hashed brown potatoes sizzled on a café stove. We were in high spirits.

Then somebody noticed that Aspenite Jim Ward, was missing. He appeared shortly. His wax had been running slow, and while he stopped to rewax, the rest of us had skied off, leaving him behind. Had he been injured or lost in bad weather, the result could have been tragic.

We made an important rule, one all ski-touring groups should make, whether they are on a day or four-day tour: two persons should always bring up the rear. The buddy system *must* be observed.

We had gone twelve miles in three hours, most of it downhill. We still had to go uphill, but it was a gradual incline. Maybe we could go farther than our preplanned eighteen miles a day. Maybe we could make it to Aspen in three days, we thought, well fueled with a hearty breakfast.

These false impressions accompanied us as we began skiing beside U.S. 24, a paved highway connecting the historic mining town of Leadville and the main road between Denver and Grand Junction.

Skiing the side of the highway, which would take us to the trail up Homestake Reservoir, and the forest beyond, proved to be a mistake. Sand and ash put down on snowy roads for tire traction and later plowed into the roadside snowbanks where we were now skiing, stripped the skis of their wax and protective pine-tar base.

We took off our skis and walked up the road. The sun was hot. Motorists gawked at this band of roving skiers: men dressed in wool caps, knickers, turtleneck T-shirts. Some appeared to be in their stocking feet, having pulled wool socks over their ski boots to keep them from becoming wet from melting snow. A car stopped, the driver apparently unable to contain his curiosity. "Where you going?" he queried.

"Aspen," I replied, trying to be as casual as possible about the whole thing.

"How?" came the next question.

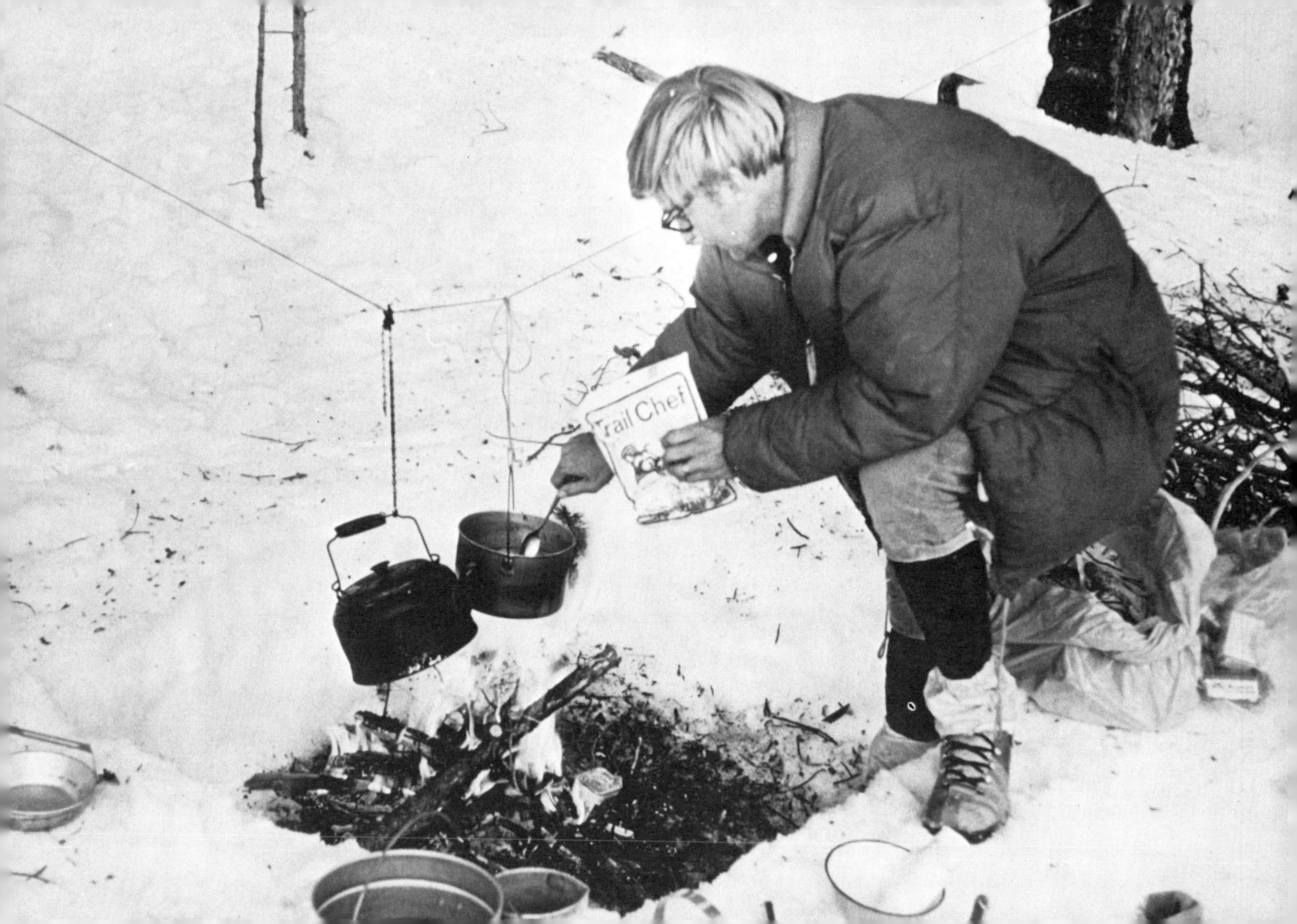
Trail Chef

"Through the mountains. Right up there." I pointed to the dark timber and high peaks beyond.

"That's pretty rough country," the man observed incredulously. "Don't you want a ride?"

I chuckled inwardly and merely shrugged a shoulder. My answer was no, and it would be useless to explain the motives, the compulsions, that drove us.

We reached the trail to Homestake Reservoir, put on our skis, and left the road, symbol of progress and link with civilization. Moving single file, we crossed a snow-covered field and entered the winter-wilderness mountains. A fence top with one strand of barbed wire dipping in and out of white fluff paralleled our trail.

The field ended in a rise to a wooded tongue of aspens that spilled onto the trail from a nearby hill. It was cooler in the shadows; we were hidden from the blistering sun. But the exercise still kept the perspiration flowing freely.

The continuous uphill climb caused tiredness to creep in softly. First, it sat on pack straps, then it moved to legs and slowed the pace. It cramped feet and clouded minds. The gradual incline was like a treadmill. It took its toll.

A lunch break, then back on the skis, through a tunnel of spruce, mouth dry, always looking for mountain streams with cold, clear water, sun sinking slowly until it was midafternoon and time to stop and make camp.

We had not made it to the reservoir or the dark timber on the far side, a destination considered feasible after breakfast. That had been a careless dream of exaltation after a long downhill run. We were exactly where we had planned to be.

Camping in the snow was pleasant, despite what one's imagination might conjure. All we had to do was to keep dry. Tents were pitched in a stand of lodgepole pines.

Aspenite Lars Larson took his shovel and dug a snow trench, which looked much like an open grave. To make it livable, he first put twigs and then a ground cover on the floor of the pit. A sleeping bag made up the rest of what Larson called home. The snow would retain body heat; the sticks and cover would act as a mattress.

We changed to dry clothes, leaving wet clothing hanging from trees like formless Raggedy Ann dolls. We built a fire and cooked dinner: freeze-dried stew and chicken Tetrazzini.

The campfire burned brightly, sending a ring of warmth into the cold night air, and a full moon came boring through the forest like a headlight on a phantom locomotive, lighting the path that coiled upward into the frozen black mountains.

We sat around the fire and retold and exaggerated our favorite stories before tired faces disappeared from the fire's glow and small flashlight beams blinked like fireflies inside tents and snow caves.

Hikers sat at the edge of their tents and removed wet boots. To stay dry, they did a backward somersault into the shelter. Inside, they undressed in their sleeping bags and organized clothes for the next day.

After just one day in the wilderness, our everyday concerns seemed to vanish. Money had no value where we were; a million dollars wouldn't have bought a cup of coffee in the wilderness. The first priority wasn't yourself but the group and its health and safety. I started to care deeply about how

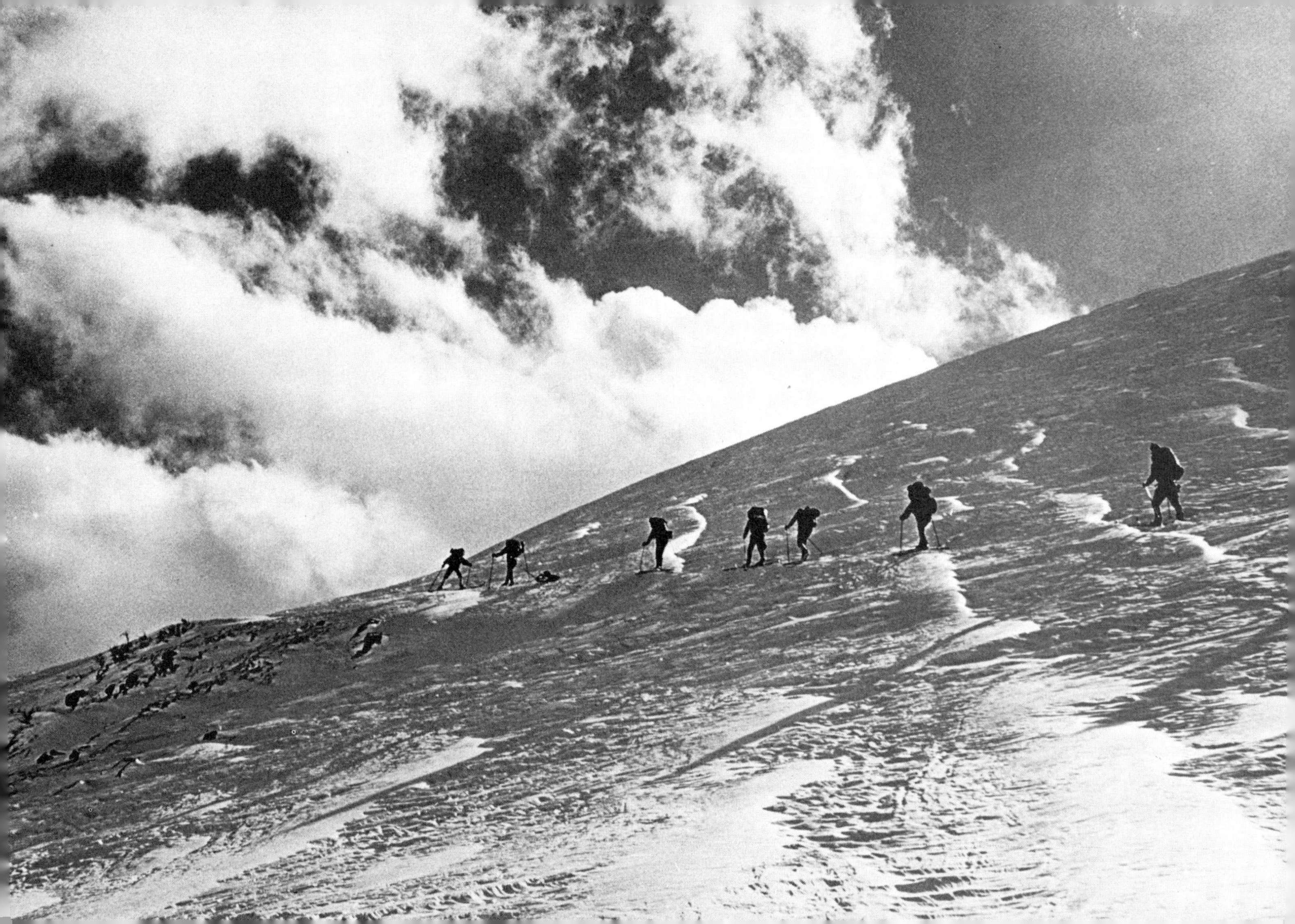

everyone was doing. This binding force manifested itself later when one man with a bad back decided to give up and return to Aspen in a helicopter with a camera crew that filmed part of the trek. His decision to fly out wasn't easy, but it was honorable, for if his back had been injured in an area inaccessible to outside help, it would have been the end of the trek and the beginning of a rescue.

We awoke in the cold predawn. Because the temperature was fifteen below, we decided to put off breakfast until the sun had warmed the countryside. We headed for the timber on the far side of Homestake Reservoir, four miles away and two thousand feet up. This could have been a mistake. By the time we reached the dam, some skiers were exhausted from lack of energy that a good breakfast might have provided. All of us were munching on snacks just to make it across the ice to the morning meal.

We skied over a small layer of snow covering the frozen reservoir. To either side were the avalanche chutes that had been visible on the Forest Service maps, and we avoided their paths as much as possible by weaving across the ice until we were out of danger.

After a leisurely breakfast, we were back on the trail, climbing slowly up the east ridge of Homestake Creek, a small stream that feeds the reservoir bearing its name. Up we went up toward the timberline at eleven thousand five hundred feet. It was hard moving. The snow was sugary and stole valuable energy by making us fight the mountain. Pole checks were difficult. Eventually everyone made it to twelve thousand seven hundred feet, for us the top of the world.

Now we could see what the "bear that went over the mountain" saw: the other side — five miles of downhill powder.

The desire to swoop downhill through the snow after our high mountain crossing was almost overwhelming. I knew it would be dangerous to gather too much speed.

One skier shot out into the untracked snow, cut a few easy turns, and undoubtably felt the intoxicating speed surround him. Going down was much better than going up.

Then, without warning, the soft powder seemed to disintegrate in mid-turn, and he was tumbling through thousands of flakes. His pack was wrenched from his back and its contents strewn over the hill — but the only injury was to his ego. This was the beginning of a run that ended at an old stone cabin wedged into Hell Gate Canyon on the Frying Pan River.

It was late afternoon when we finally saw the small hut. "First come, first served," someone yelled, and an instant replay of the Oklahoma Land Rush began. Skiers peeled off down an old railroad grade in a race for a place in the shelter.

Some fell, others slid or rolled, but eventually all were packed inside like sardines. Extra food, carried in case a snowstorm had held up our trip on the other side of the mountain, was broken out. There wasn't any need to save it now, and the result was a six-course meal, including cheesecake, which we ate with breakfast.

The next morning we skied down the old Colorado Midland Railroad bed, followed meadows and creeks, went up an unmapped Bureau of Reclamation road, and stopped on Mt. Porphyry.

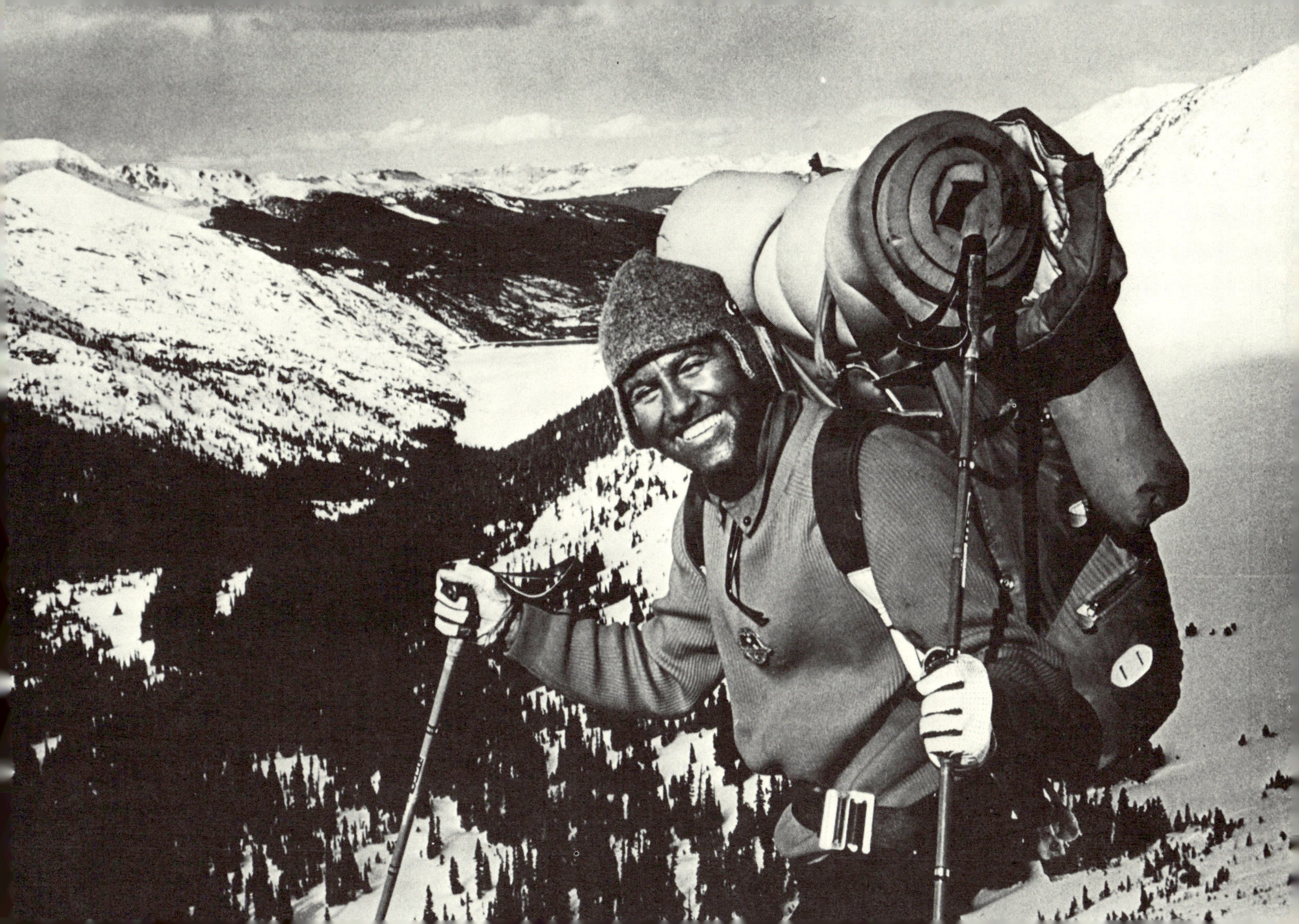

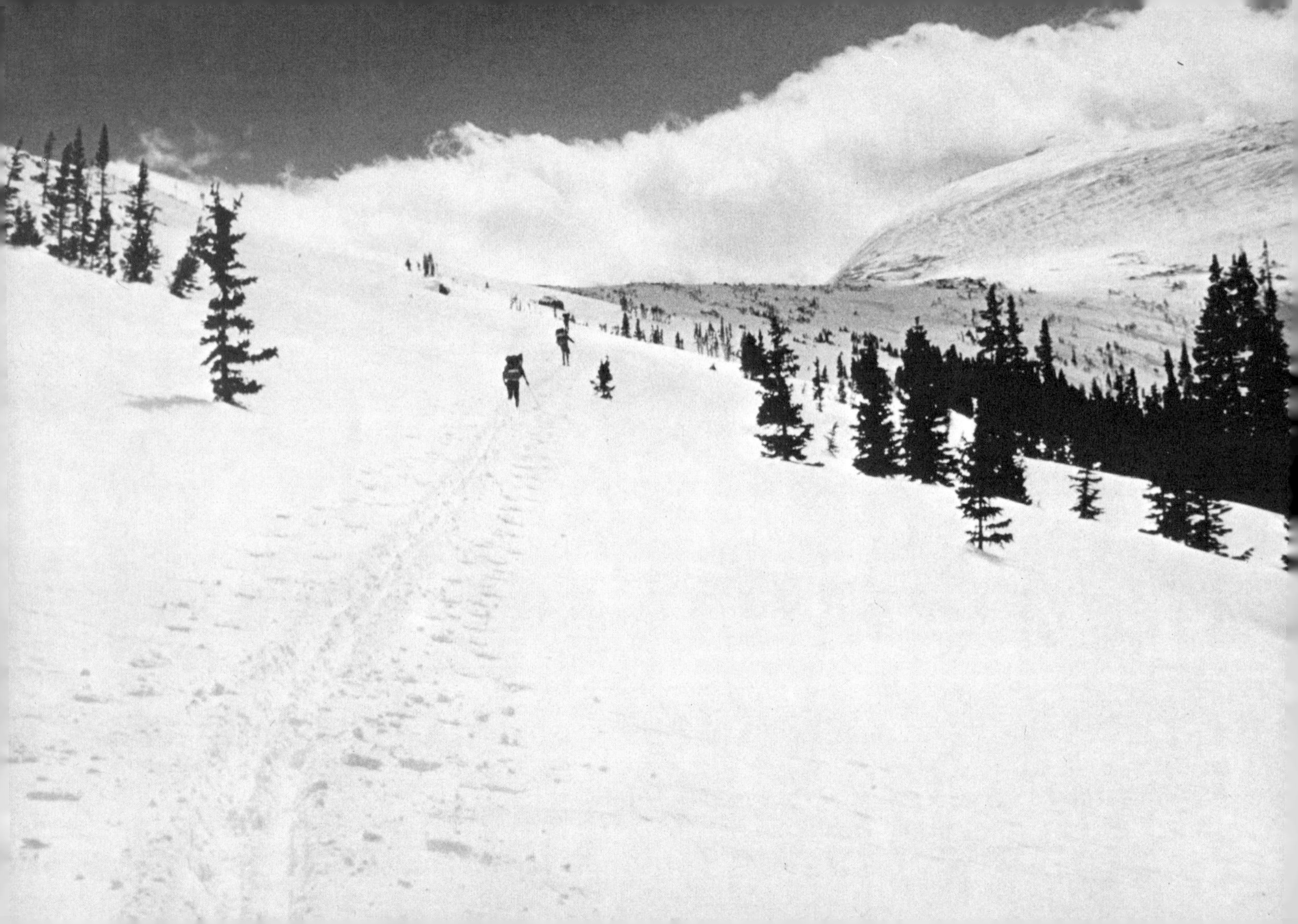

The trek from the cabin to the north face of Mt. Porphyry was exhausting. It was 4:30 P.M. when we pitched camp in a stand of Colorado blue spruce.

A skier who had gotten his feet wet from melting snow feared frostbite as the evening chill set in. He ate dinner quickly and crawled into his sleeping bag. His toes were white with the first sign of "the bite." "I feel safe here," he said as he began to warm.

Inside my tent, nestled in a grove of pine trees, with needled boughs like woolly arms cradling my wilderness home, I was soon asleep.

The next morning we awoke with the excitement of completing the tour. We nibbled on a breakfast of dried fruit, coconut, nuts and chocolate — the mixture called "gorp"— drank tea, and headed for Aspen.

Thick forests marked the way, a mass of greenery against the white snow and gray, overcast sky. As we skied toward the trees, they would fan apart and become individual aspen, Engelmann spruce, pine, and Colorado blue spruce.

"That's Red Mountain just across there," someone said.

Aspen was on the other side of Red Mountain. It looked close. We continued our traverse, laughing and joking and pointing to the mountain. We thought we had it made. But the traverse ended abruptly when we came to a steep ice wall that dropped four hundred feet into upper Woody Creek, a tangle of thick forest and felled timber.

"I thought we went downhill all the way to Aspen," Tony Tafel, my assistant said. Another skier looked at his broken binding, which had been wired together, and glanced at the gorge to be crossed.

We picked our way down the steep hillside — slipping, sliding, and grabbing trees to slow the descent, and ate our last lunch by the running brook in a part of the mountains that few people see. Possibly the best way to get to it is as we did, in winter on skis. It would be a hard summer walk.

After lunch, we followed an unnamed creek to Horse Park. The trail wound through mysterious woods piled deep with wind-sculptured snow. Bridges of snow rested on fallen trees that spanned the creek. Mushrooms of snow appeared on tree stumps. The place was quiet except for an occasional whisper of wind scraping through the trees and over the ground.

From Horse Park, it was a twenty-nine-hundred-foot drop to Aspen, covering eight miles down Hunter Creek. We would be in Aspen by 4 P.M.

Mt. Massive (one of Colorado's highest at fourteen thousand three hundred and fifty feet) was blanketed by storm-heavy clouds. A front was closing in, but we would beat it home.

The trip was over, but it wasn't the end for members of the group. The memories of the struggle up steep terrain and the smooth runs through bowls of deep powder would long be remembered.

In the wilderness we had to work together as a team. This effort gave each man a realistic set of life values to measure his life style against.

These basic values of survival created a spirit similar to what I encountered as an international competitor, but on a noncompetitive scale.

Petty differences were discarded in an effort to live. It is sad this same spirit does not accompany our everyday living. Maybe someday everyone will get a chance to experience this basic life struggle and find success on this level.

Epilogue

As an adventure, our trip of course doesn't compare in magnitude with such great expeditions as those across Greenland in the 1870s, or the trans-Scandinavian treks a decade later. But it was significant to us, for it demonstrated that adventures in the winter wilderness are not limited to explorers alone but open to any competent skier.

Our group consisted of an electrician who is now a shopkeeper, real estate brokers, a contractor, a hotel clerk, ski-touring instructors, Alpine ski instructors, and a newspaperman. What we had in common was a desire for an adventure on our level and a hankering to test ourselves in another environment.

Touring lets you do this whether you go three miles or thirty miles into the wilderness, and ordinary people are now making journeys like ours every winter, using the skills and technique presented in this book.

Bibliography

American National Red Cross. *First Aid Textbook.* Garden City, New York: Doubleday, 1957.

Angier, Bradford. *Skills for Taming the Wilds.* New York: Pocket Books, 1972.

Baldwin, Edward R. *The Cross-Country Skiing Handbook.* New York: Charles Scribner's, 1972.

Brady, Michael. *Nordic Touring and Cross-Country Skiing.* Oslo, Norway: Dreyers Forlag, 1971.

Caldwell, John. *The New Cross-Country Ski Book.* Brattleboro, Vermont: The Stephen Greene Press, 1971.

Lederer, William J., and Wilson, Joe Pete. *Complete Cross-Country Skiing and Ski-Touring.* New York: W. W. Norton, 1970.

Lund, Morton. *The Pleasures of Cross-Country Skiing.* New York: Outerbridge & Lazard, 1972.

Lunn, Arnold. *The Complete Ski-Runner.* New York: Charles Scribner's, 1931.

Osgood, William E., and Hurley, Leslie J. *Ski-Touring: An Introductory Guide.* Rutland, Vermont: Charles E. Tuttle, 1969.

Strode, Hudson. *Sweden: Model for a World.* New York: Harcourt, Brace, 1949.

Tejada-Flores, Lito, and Steck, Allen. *Wilderness Skiing.* San Francisco: Sierra Club, 1972.

United States Department of Agriculture (Soil Conservation Service). *Snow-Survey Safety Guide.* Agric. Handbook No. 137, Washington, D.C.: Government Printing Office, 1958.

——— . *Snow Avalanches: A Handbook of Forecasting and Control Measures.* Agric. Handbook No. 194, Washington, D.C.: Government Printing Office, 1961.

United States Ski Association, Rocky Mountain Division. *Ski-Touring Instructors' Manual.* Denver: RMD-USSA, Ski-Touring Instructors' Certification Subcommittee, 1972.

Appendix

Mike Elliott, Olympic cross-country runner, displays excellent style and technique.

Sources of Information about Touring

If you want a professional eye to judge your skiing, you might be interested in touring lessons. There are numerous schools around the country and more are appearing every year. Several organizations can tell you where they are located and also provide other valuable information.

One of the best sources is the United States Ski Association (USSA), which has nine geographic divisions across the country: Eastern (USSA), 20 Main Street, Littleton, New Hampshire, 03561; Southern (USSA), P.O. Box 918, Winston-Salem, North Carolina, 27102; Central (USSA), 4437 First Avenue South, Minneapolis, Minnesota, 55409; Rocky Mountain (USSA), Suite 300, 1726 Champa Street, Denver, Colorado, 80202; Intermountain (USSA), 19 East Second South, Salt Lake City, Utah, 84111; Northern (USSA), 1111 North Seventh Avenue, Bozeman, Montana, 59715; Far West (USSA), 812 Howard Street, San Francisco, California, 94103; Pacific Northwest (USSA), P.O. Box 6228, Seattle, Washington, 98188; Alaskan (USSA), P.O. Box 4-2126, Anchorage, Alaska, 99509.

The Rocky Mountain Division was the first to have a certification program (starting in 1970) for testing potential ski-touring instructors.

Certified instructors in the RMD of the USSA must know the basic information in this book, especially beginning technique, first aid, use of map and compass, and leadership. With more and more people skiing into the backcountry, knowledge of survival skills is paramount. This is where a little technique can go a long way, especially knowing how to conserve energy, knowing when to turn back, and learning how to watch for storms.

I strongly believe that if you take lessons, your instructor should cover in some proficient manner the essentials of ski-touring as well as downhill skiing. I don't believe it is important to teach a particular "style" of ski-touring, as such. Style should be left up to the individual, who should ski in the most efficient and comfortable way for him. What is important is to establish instructor credentials to benefit students.

You might be interested in knowing what it takes to become a certified instructor in the RMD. Those who want to be certified must first complete the division's basic ski-touring course and pass a written examination. The RMD program isn't easy. Of some one hundred twenty aspirants to apprenticeship for the 1972–73 season, only about forty-five made it.

Those who succeed receive the title of Apprentice Instructor, which entitles them to teach basic technique and lead day tours. The initiates then have to complete a trial period of instruction in which they are rated by students. Only then does the RMD recognize them as Certified Instructors.

Book as an Instructors' Manual

As a matter of fact, this book can be used as an instructors' manual, either for those already teaching or for people interested in teaching touring. It can also be used as a guide for establishing a ski-touring or certification program.

I hope in the future touring, like Alpine skiing, will have a nationwide certification program for two basic reasons: to provide students with proper touring instruction and to be a source of information about the winter woods and its pleasures and dangers.

Other Information Centers

Here are a few more information centers where you can obtain data on tours, races and lessons: The American Ski-Touring Council, Inc., West Hill Road, Troy, Vermont, 05868; The New York Ski-Touring Council, Inc., Room 727, 342 Madison Avenue, New York, New York, 10017 (both have a ski-touring guide for a small price); and NASTAR (National Standard Races), World Wide Ski Corporation, 240 Madison Avenue, New York, New York, 10016 (or 2305 Canyon Boulevard, Boulder, Colorado, 80302).

Ski-Touring Races

Ski-touring races are becoming very popular in the United States. These races, also known as citizen cross-country races, are held on courses approximately eight miles long. All finishers are given some sort of recognition, for to finish is the real objective of a touring race, while the usually longer cross-country ski race rewards only the fastest finishers.

Citizen races can be for the whole family. Many competitions have up to twenty-four different classes for contestants. You are bound to fit into one of them, and you won't race alone. A Le Mans or shotgun start is used, sending everyone off at the same time. Sound like fun? It can be!

The North Star Ski-Touring Club of Minneapolis, Minnesota, hosted more than a thousand skiers for its touring race in 1972. The Colorado Gold Rush Ski-Touring Race, which begins on a lake and goes for six miles, has some seven hundred men, women and children contestants. Sweden's Vasaloppet, a fifty-mile contest for both cross-country racers and ski-touring enthusiasts, has some nine thousand skiers starting together.

Citizen races are springing up all over the country and to list all of them here would be difficult. Some of the better known include:

The Washington's Birthday Ski-Touring Race, run near the Putney School, Vermont, on the Sunday closest to Washington's birthday. For information, write: Washington's Birthday Tour Race Committee, c/o The Putney School, Putney, Vermont, 05346.

The Stowe Derby, run in February near Stowe, Vermont. For information, write: Stowe Derby Race Committee, c/o Stowe School, Stowe, Vermont, 05672.

The Madonna Vasa, held the first Sunday in March to coincide with the Vasaloppet in Sweden, and run between Madonna Mountain, Jeffersonville, Vermont, and Underhill Center. For information, write: Dr. John Bland, Upper Valley Road, Cambridge, Vermont, 05444.

The V-J-C Ski-Touring Race, run in February outside Minneapolis.

John Lindstrom, of Dundee, Illinois, runs in a touring race just for the fun of it.

For information, write: North Star Ski-Touring Club, 4231 Oakdale Avenue, Minneapolis, Minnesota, 55416.

The Colorado Gold Rush Ski-Touring Race, run near Dillon and Breckenridge. For information, write: Frisco Chamber of Commerce, Frisco, Colorado, 80433.

The Keystone Cross-Country Caper, run at Keystone Ski Area in Colorado. For information, write: Keystone Cross-Country Caper, Keystone Ski Area, Keystone, Colorado, 80433.

Yosemite Ski-Touring Race, run in California. For information, write: Yosemite Mountaineering School, Yosemite National Park, California, 95389. For other California events, write: Cal-Nordic Ski-Touring Center, Tamarack Lodge, Mammoth Lakes, California, 93546.

The John Craig Memorial Ski-Touring Race, run in Oregon in April in remembrance of pioneer ski mailmen. Contestants carry a sack of mail during the race. For information, write: Oregon Nordic Club, Bend, Oregon, 97701.

Fairbanks Skiathon, run near Fairbanks, Alaska, to coincide with the vernal equinox (mid-March). For information, write: Nordic Ski Club of Fairbanks, Fairbanks, Alaska, 99701. This group also hosts the Glacier Stampede, held at the end of April.

There are several Canadian touring races, also. Information on these can be obtained by writing to the Canadian Ski Association, Room C-15, 306 Place d'Youville, Montreal 125, Quebec.

If you have questions about ski areas, the ski patrol or the ski industry, you can write: National Ski Areas Association, 369 Lexington Avenue, New York, New York, 10017; The National Ski Patrol System, Inc., 2901 Sheridan Boulevard, Denver, Colorado, 80214; or Ski Industries America, 432 Park Avenue South, New York City, New York, 10016.

Warm-up Exercises

The amount of effort expended to cover a given distance not only has a great deal to do with your ability to ski and the wax, equipment and clothing you use, but also on your physical condition.

A person in average health can go on a day trip, but the better shape he is in, the higher the chances he will ski better. Good shape improves performance in most sports.

To loosen those tight muscles before going out to ski, try these ten quick exercises. They should take only five or ten minutes and will help prevent possible injury.

Head Rolling: Standing in a normal, relaxed position, rotate your head slowly in a wide circle. Do this approximately five times to the right and then reverse direction. Roll your head slowly.

Shoulder Rolling and Swinging: Standing with your arms straight out in front of you, roll *just* your shoulders about seven times before reversing direction. Hold your arms out to the side, shoulder-high, and make small circles with your hands and arms about seven times, first towards your back and then in the opposite direction. Now, swing one arm at a time in a wide circle frontward and backward. Start slow and relaxed and gradually increase the speed.

Side Bending: Stand in a straddle position (feet spread about three feet), put your hands on your hips, and slowly bob twice to each side: straight to the side, not forward. Move your hands to your shoulders and repeat the same exercise; then move your hands overhead and repeat. Now work back down: hands on shoulders, hips, and then hanging loosely by your side.

Trunk Twist: Assume a straddle position with hands on hips and make a circle, rolling the upper body in a clockwise direction by bending forward, then to the side, then back and then to the other side. Do it four times. Now reverse the direction. This should be done slowly and in as wide a circle as possible.

Half Deep-Knee Bend: Standing straight, hands on hips, squat so the thigh is parallel to the floor. Hold that position approximately ten seconds and then stand up and shake each leg to relax the muscles. Repeat this five times.

Hands-on-Floor Stand-up: From a standing position, crouch down so you can place your hands flat on the floor just in front of your feet. Now, keeping your hands flat, try to straighten your legs until you feel the leg muscles begin to pull slightly. Bob up and down in this position two or three times and then return to a low crouch. Repeat this movement about four times, and then stand up and shake each leg to relax the muscles.

Leg over Leg: Lie on your stomach with your hands under your chin. With a straight leg, reach over and across the other leg as far as possible, making sure your elbows and chest remain on the floor at all times. When the leg is stretched as far as possible, bob it twice. Do this about four times with each leg.

Hurdle Exercise: Sit on the floor in a hurdler's position: one leg and foot straight out in front, the other bent to the side behind you. Clasp your hands behind your head. Now bob twice towards the straight leg and then twice towards the bent leg. Do this four times and then switch leg positions and repeat the exercise.

Leg Stretchers: Stand in a straddle position (legs fore and aft). Put the front foot against a wall with the heel on the floor as close to the wall as possible. Bend the back leg. Put hands on hips. Keeping the front leg straight at all times, use the back leg to bob forward, stretching the muscles of the forward leg. Bob six times and then shake the front leg to relax the muscles. Repeat the exercise with the opposite leg. Next, assume the original position, only this time, bend the knee of the forward leg towards the wall in a bobbing motion, stretching the muscles in the lower leg and ankle. Bob six times and switch to the other leg.

Side-Straddle Hop: From a standing position, arms at your side, jump to a side-straddle position (legs spread to the sides) while swinging your arms straight overhead. Immediately jump back to a normal standing position. The next jump should put the legs in a straddle position fore and aft while swinging the arms to the same position. Again return to a normal standing position. Repeat this four-count exercise eight times.

Preseason Conditioning

Generally speaking, active summer and fall sports that you enjoy doing are very good to tone your muscles for ski-touring. Some of my favorites are bicycling, soccer, tennis, gymnastics, and day or weekend hikes.

Here are a few more hints to improve your physical condition. Be regular with some kind of exercise program, whether it be conditioning exercises or a sport.

Exercising three times a week is ideal, so you can alternate a day of exercise with a day of rest. And don't overdo it: an hour of vigorous exercise is plenty.

If you are interested in improving your physical health, then push yourself *just a little* each time out. Before you take part in *any* active sport I suggest you do the ten warm-up exercises described above to stretch the muscles, which will help prevent any possible injury.

Three Special Suggestions for Ski-Touring

For Balance: Exercises that will help your balance are good for ski-touring. Here are a few to try: walk on a guardrail or railroad track for distance, ride a unicycle, do handstands, balance objects — a pole on your chin, for example, or a folding chair on two fingers, or bounce a ball on your forehead.

Chair Sit: This leg-strengthening exercise is done by sitting in an imaginary chair, your back against a wall. Find a wall you can lean against, then slide down it to a "sitting" position. Your lower legs should be vertical, your thighs parallel to the floor. Your back must be pressed flat against the wall and your arms folded or hanging loose at your sides, but not touching your legs at any time.

When your legs feel like they are starting to "burn" from tiredness, stand up and shake the muscles loose to relax them. Do this exercise once more. Keep track of how long you can sit, and measure your progress by the clock.

You may start out doing this for only fifteen seconds, but when you are in good shape you can last four minutes.

This exercise not only will strengthen your thighs but also will give you practice in bending your knees. If you ever want to be a good skier, you will need the strength to keep your knees bent while skiing.

Telemark Jump: When skiing with a loose-heel binding, it is important to be able to perform the telemark position automatically. To acquire this skill takes practice, which can be done on dry land without skis.

From a standing position, crouch and jump straight up. Keep your legs and feet together to the top of the jump. *Only* on the way down should the legs split into a telemark position.

If you do that ten times a day during the fall, it will help you immensely with your telemark when skiing starts.

If you have gotten a spur-of-the-moment invitation to go touring next weekend and want to tone your muscles a little, or if you want to get ready for the winter season, try these simple exercises.

Good skiing!

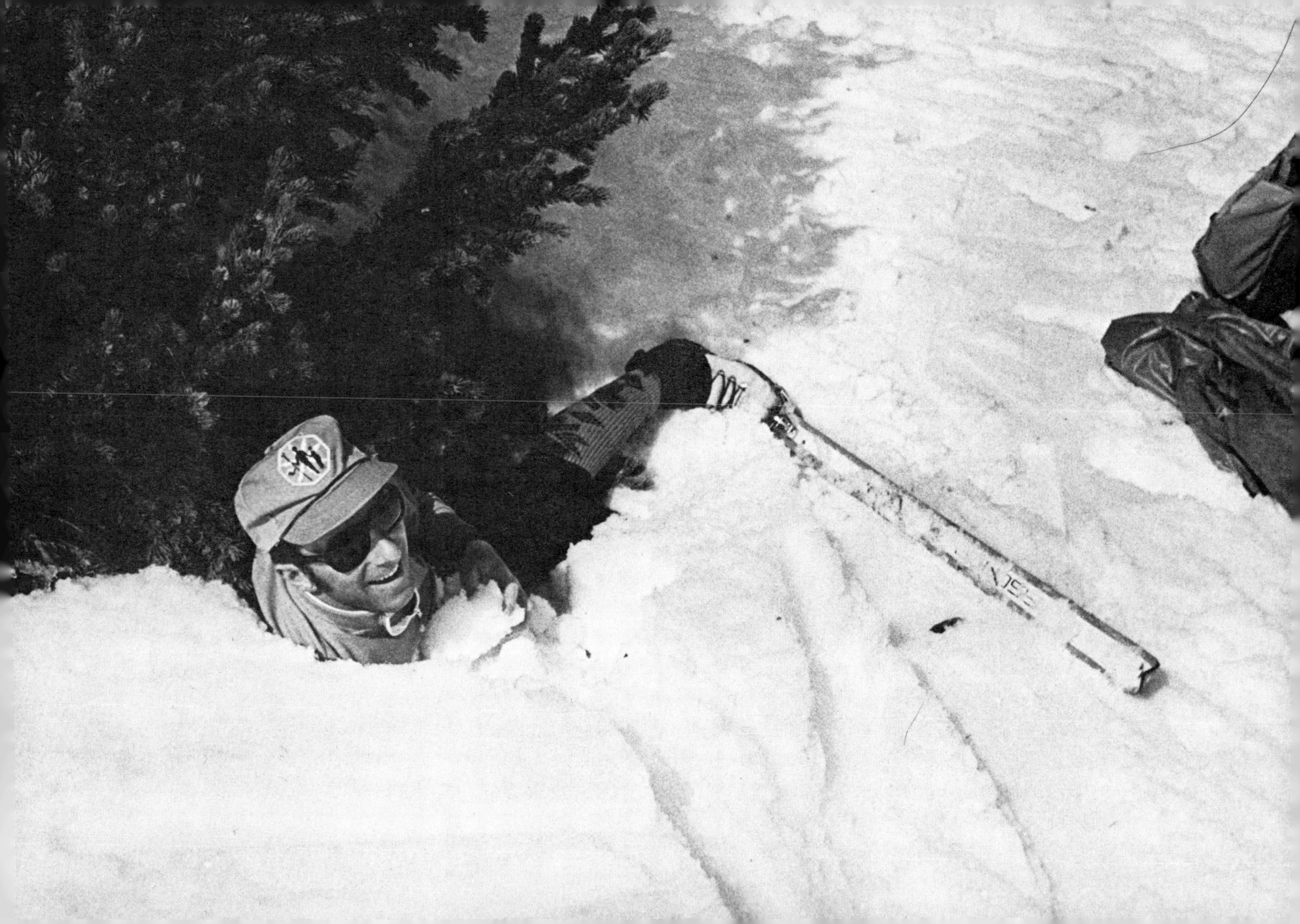

Illustration Credits

Photos by Steve Rieschl: 2, 5 (*upper left*), 9, 20, 22, 23, 109, 110 (*bottom*), 114, 116, 162, 171, 176 (*right*), 181, 183, 185, 187, 188, 201

Photos by Peter Runyon: 5 (*lower right*), 31 (*bottom*), 76, 82, 83, 89, 110 (*top*), 138, 140, 147, 148, 149, 152, 153, 154, 159, 166, 203

Photos by Balfanz: 5 (*lower left*), 5 (*upper right*), 196

Photos by Steve Larson: 6, 163, 166, 176 (*left*)

Photo by Helmut Kain, Mitterndorf, Austria: 7

Photos by Bill Herbeck, Stott Shot/Vail: 8, 113

Photos by Stott Shot/Vail: 24, 27, 28, 29, 31 (*top*), 34, 35, 36, 37, 38, 39, 41, 42, 43, 44, 45, 46, 47, 48, 49, 50, 51, 52, 53, 54, 57, 58, 59, 64, 65, 66, 67, 68, 69, 70, 71, 72, 73, 77, 80, 81, 84, 85, 86, 87, 88, 90, 91, 92, 93, 108, 119, 120, 121, 123, 132, 135, 141, 142, 143, 145, 150, 151, 156, 158, 199

Photo by Dave Pratt: 155